PROBE Bible Study
Psalm 1

with Matthew Henry's Commentary

Large Print 16 point

Paula Nafziger

King James Today™

Title..............................PROBE Bible Study Psalm 1
Subtitle ....with Matthew Henry's Commentary
....Large Print — 16 point, King James Today™
Series ....19001 (19th book of the Bible, Chapter 1)
Type.......................................Trade Paperback (US), Large Print
AU Prepared for Publication ...Paula Nafziger, Chaplain   ©2021 Paula Nafziger
ISBN-13 978-1948136853   9 8 7 6 5 4 3

All scripture is from an easier-to-read King James Version, King James Today™
Cover—Scripture Application: "I will instruct you and teach you in the way which you shall go: I will guide you with my eye." Psalm 32:8 Art by Mari Dein

Other books available for purchase Online or at your favorite bookstore:

123 PRAY guides you through a simple devotional plan to read a chapter of the Bible (your choice), focus on one or more verses, write them out, acknowledge what God places upon your heart, then PRAY! This prayer journal gives you prompts to encourage real and intimate communication with the Lord. Use this book to begin or continue a daily habit of time in His word, followed by prayer. It includes • A brief review on prayer to "talk to God" personally and on paper • Easy-to-use journal forms to keep you focused on growing • Dragonfly & damselfly facts with "stress-less" coloring pages • Large Print 18 point.

Grow Time WORD Journals encourage you to write a verse you find interesting, pay attention to details you choose to research, then formulate personal application. • Large Print 18 point.

- Grow Time 365 The Bible
- Grow Time 364 Old Testament
- Grow Time 260 New Testament
- Grow Time 249 Historical Books
- Grow Time 243 Poetry/Wisdom
- Grow Time 187 Law/Torah
- Grow Time 183 Major Prophets
- Grow Time 180 WORD Journal

- Grow Time 150 Psalms
- Grow Time 117 Gospels & Acts
- Grow Time 87 Paul's Letters
- Grow Time 67 Minor Prophets
- Grow Time 56 Letters & Prophecy
- Grow Time 31 Proverbs
- Grow Time 12 12 Months in Proverbs

Read, Write & REAP Bible Study System: **R**ead the chapter, choose a verse or two to hand copy, then re-write from a different translation, **E**xamine the text using your favorite resources, **A**cknowledge what God prompts your heart to act upon, attest to personal experiences, then "talk to God" in written **P**rayer.   • Large Print 18 point.

PROBE Bible Study–Psalm 1   Table of Contents

N.T. Key: Direct speaking of Christ appear in *italics*. Quotation of Christ, God,
The Holy Spirit, Their messengers, or the Old Testament, appear in *italic underlined*.
The Bible in its entirety is the word of God.

King James Today™

What makes this contemporary King James Version easier-to-read?

• Unnecessary word endings "est, eth, st, th, and ith" are dropped, **e.g.,** build<u>est</u> (build), build<u>eth</u> (builds), do<u>st</u> (do), lie<u>th</u> (lie), sa<u>ith</u> (says).

• Old English is replaced **e.g.,** art (are), hither (here), nigh (near), oft (often), thee (you), thine (your), thou (you), thy (your) thyself (yourself), unto (to), wast (were), ye (you).

• Old English spelling is updated **e.g.,** labour (labor), licence (license), musick (music), publick (public), shew (show), wilt (will).

• Ye, you, you-ward, your, yours, and yourselves, referring to more than one person, is noted by a superscript ^{P} (for plural) **e.g.,** you^P.

• Spelling consistency for proper nouns **e.g.,** Balac (Balak), Elias (Elijah), Esaias (Isaiah), Jonas (Jonah), Noe (Noah), Osee (Hosea), Sion (Zion).

Comparison of scripture:
King **J**ames **V**ersion (KJV) versus **K**ing **J**ames **T**oday™ (KJT):

> Blessed is the man that walketh not in the counsel of the ungodly, nor standeth in the way of sinners, nor sitteth in the seat of the scornful. Psalm 1:1 **KJV**

> Blessed is the man that walks not in the counsel of the ungodly, nor stands in the way of sinners, nor sits in the seat of the scornful. Psalm 1:1 **KJT**

To the right is a popular verse within Psalm 1 but not necessarily the theme or vital verse of the book or chapter.

RenewingLives.com

For the LORD
knows the way of
the righteous: but
the way
of the ungodly
shall perish.

Psalm 1:6

What does it mean to probe? It means to search and explore thoroughly, to make a penetrating or critical investigation.

The **PROBE** Bible study method helps you seek and find knowledge from details in the Bible. You'll discover truth *[the real state of things]* by comparing facts, considering actions and circumstances, asking questions to find meaning and answers, investigating the contents, and weighing arguments to form a correct judgment or opinion.

Studying the Bible begins with a desire to study *[to fix the mind or dwell in deep thought upon a subject for the purpose of learning and understanding]*. It takes effort *[strenuous exertion to accomplish an endeavor]* to search the scriptures for details and time to observe and prove truth.

The steps of the **PROBE** Bible study method are:

1) **P**ray it *[connect and exchange thoughts with God]*

2) **R**ead it *[understand written words and ideas]*

3) **O**bserve it *[take notice of events, facts, and principles]*

4) **B**ack-it-up *[prove truth]*. This is done by **examination** *[inquiry into circumstances, facts, and truth]*, using a variety of resources, *i.e.,* ancient maps, Bible commentaries, concordances, cross-references, dictionaries, encyclopedias, historical documents, interlinear Bibles, lectures, lexicons, teachings, etc. Reliable resources pave the way to a reasonable **interpretation** *[unfolding what is not understood or obvious]*. Then you can form an educated **judgment** *[the determination of the mind formed from comparing the relations of ideas, or the comparison of facts and arguments to ascertain truth]*, or **opinion** *[the decision the mind forms of truth or falsehood which is supported by a degree of evidence that renders it probable but does not produce absolute knowledge or certainty]*.

5) **E**xpress it *[make your feelings, opinions, and passions known by your actions, behavior, course of life, leadership, and words]*. Respond to God's word as your understanding increases. **Acknowledge** what you sense God wants you to do. **Apply** God's word to your life and circumstances. **Share** personal experiences that bear witness and support what you've learned. **Be creative** in expressing what God impresses upon your heart. Determine **goals**, make **plans**, and **evaluate** your progress.

About this workbook:

Definition note: To make sure you know what words in this workbook mean, you will find definitions shown in brackets after the word. Here is an example: Reading requires cognitive *[conscious intellectual activity such as thinking, reasoning, remembering]* mental action.

If you find it difficult to read a sentence that contains a definition, simply read the sentence again, but skip over the definition by ignoring the bracketed portion. While it saves time to know the meaning of a word without referring to a dictionary or the back of the book, having a definition inserted into a sentence makes the sentence harder to read, takes extra effort, and is visually busy. The benefit of making sure you know the definition of a word outweighs the difficulty of getting used to reading it within the sentence.

Forms note: This workbook contains many forms that can be used for classwork, home-school assignments, and small group bible study, in addition to your own personal study.

Photocopy permission: You have permission to photocopy pages within this book for non-commercial use. This means you cannot charge a person to receive or obtain any portion of this book above the paper's actual cost and copy charge. This is allowed to encourage others to learn how to study the Bible. For example, a teacher can photocopy pages and give them to their students. A church, Bible study group, or leader can copy some or all of the book and give it to congregants (but not at a profit). Jail/Prison Chaplains can give out pages to inmates, and so on. You will most likely find it is easier to have the book intact and cost-prohibitive to photocopy it as a whole unless you are privy to free photocopy options at your facility.

Disassembly to photocopy: Our publisher does not offer tear out page options at this time. If you find photocopying beneficial, you will need to cut pages at the inside margin or remove them by hand disassembly:

1) Beginning at the **back cover,** slowly tear off the cover, then every <u>single</u> page *slowly* at an angle. Try to tear each page at the glue edge as cleanly as possible. If you are impatient and remove multiple pages, you'll end up with a mess! Remove the glue residue from the book edge often.

RenewingLives.com

About this study:

The PROBE Bible Study method is very detailed yet provides maximum flexibility. If you are in a class or group, your teacher/leader will assign pages to be completed in their preferred order. If you are studying independently, you'll need to decide on the pages you want to complete and in which order. Most forms appear in alphabetical order for easy reference.

The ultimate goal of this study is for you to begin or continue studying the Bible to uncover details that help you understand God's message to mankind. *God is in the details!*

The Bible was originally penned in Aramaic, Greek, and Hebrew. Knowing the biblical languages would really benefit a student of the Bible. Because the Bible was translated into English, grammar is shown throughout this workbook. You will likely find your English grammar and understanding of word definitions improves just by doing this study.

Because the PROBE Bible Study method works for any book or chapter of the Bible, there might pages that do not apply to the book/chapter/verse you are focusing on. Simply skip those pages.

The PROBE Bible Study method could keep you busy in the Bible for weeks or months, depending on how much time you invest in learning. Spending a long time in an exhaustive study of only one chapter of the Bible might seem crazy, but if you submit yourself to this style of learning, memorization of the information will occur naturally. You will likely gain insight that is missed in comparison to easy, quick, or superficial studies. The Holy Spirit will speak to your heart/mind as you dwell in His word. Don't loose track of the fact that the book, chapter, or verse you study is connected to the context of the Bible as a whole.

Your investment of time in the study of God's word will bring not only knowledge but should also cause you to grow in wisdom. You can expect to be changed inside and out by the word of the living God.

"All scripture is given by inspiration of God, and is profitable for doctrine, for reproof, for correction, for instruction in righteousness: That the man of God may be perfect, thoroughly furnished to all good works." 2 Timothy 3:16-17

Pray it Read it Observe it Back it up Express it

This book is formatted to give you ideas of what you can use and do to study one chapter of the Psalms at a time. It provides prompts to answer the basics of Bible study such as: who, what, where, when, why, and how. The biblical text is usually displayed with wide margins and lines so you can write out God's word or insert your study notes. Study pages and WORD Journals provide a way to record what you learn as you spend time in God's word.

The Book of Psalms is the most ancient collection of poetry in the world. Set to music, it served as the hymnbook for the Israelites and early church in praise and worship of YHVH, the LORD. Rather than rhythm and rhyme, it uses clarification, contrasts, comparisons, and repetition. The Psalms have provided comfort, encouragement, and strength for over a thousand years.

Stress-less Coloring

Coloring isn't just for kids. Adults need to unplug and unwind too! Coloring is an artistic expression anyone can enjoy.

A coloring page provides an outline that you, the artist, fill with the use of crayons, markers, paint, pens, or pencils. Beautiful display-worthy results can be accomplished by shading with a simple lead pencil.

Coloring is proven to be therapeutic *[having beneficial effects on the body or mind]*. Coloring enthusiasts find the decisions, details, patterns, and repetition reduce anxiety and stress. By calming your thoughts as you focus on the current activity, the cares of the day are less likely to consume your attention.

The coloring pages within this book are provided to help you stress less. By mixing it up between reading, meditating on God's word, and coloring, you'll keep "Busy in the Bible."™

Why should you color? *Because it's healthy old fashioned fun!*

Psalm or Psalms?

Psalms refer to a collection of 150 individual writings, each known as a Psalm, e.g., Psalm 1 from The Book of Psalms. When referring to a particular Psalm, the word is singular.

Superscriptions

The beginning of Psalm 3 introduces a "superscription." A superscription is defined as *[that which is written or engraved on the outside or above something else.]* For example, U.S. coins include a superscription "In God We Trust."

Jewish people who do not read Hebrew commonly use "The Holy Scriptures" 1917 JPS (Jewish Publication Society) version of the Masoretic Hebrew manuscripts. It is an authoritative translation from the original Hebrew into English. Non-Jewish people (Gentiles) and Jews who accept the Old and New Testament as the complete word of God commonly use "The Holy Bible."

Verse numbers in "The Holy Scriptures" may differ from the verse numbers in "The Holy Bible" because The Holy Scriptures list superscriptions as separate verses. Most translations of The Holy Bible list the superscription as a title/heading before the remaining verses, or include them as part of the initial verse itself, and begin numbering the verses after the superscription.

Superscriptions are recorded in one hundred and sixteen of the one hundred and fifty Psalms. They name the author or the instrument, provide musical style or notations, give direction to the musician, describe the subject, occasion, or circumstances surrounding the composition, and other descriptive information. The authority of superscriptions is disputed by some biblical scholars.

Hebrew Acrostics

An acrostic is *[an arrangement of words in a text or verse in which the first letter(s) of the lines, taken in order, form the name of a person, the subject of a composition, a title, motto, word, phrase, pattern, or an alphabetical arrangement].* It is believed the use of acrostics assisted with mnemonic *[assisting the memory].* Poems that consist of detached thoughts on a subject might include an acrostic.

# of verses each Hebrew consonant covers in "acrostic Psalms:"

Psalm 9-10	25	34	37	111	112	119	145
2	1	1	2	1/2	1/2	8	1

The Hebrew alphabet consists of 22 letters—all of them consonants—all uppercase letters, no punctuation. Hebrew reads RIGHT to left.

Approximate Modern Israeli pronunciation:

HEH	DAH-leht	GEE-mehl	BEHT	AH-lehf
ה 5	ד 4	ג 3	ב 2	א 1
He	Dalet	Gimel	Bet	Alef

YOOD	THET	KHEHT	ZAH-yeen	VAHV
י 10	ט 9	ח 8	ז 7	ו 6
Yod	Tet	Het	Zayin	Vav

SAH-mehkh	NOON	MEHM	LAH-mehd	KHAHF
ס 15	נ 14	מ 13	ל 12	כ 11
Samekh	Nun	Mem	Lamed	Kaf

REHSH	KOOF	TSAH-dee	PEH	AH-yeen
ר 20	ק 19	צ 18	פ 17	ע 16
Resh	Qof	Tsadi	Pe	Ayin

	TAHV	SHEEN		
	ת 22	ש 21		
	Tav	Shin		

Hebrew Alphabet

Examples:
ALPHABET HEBREW THE
—LETTERS 22 OF CONSISTS
—CONSONANTS THEM OF ALL
LETTERS UPPERCASE ALL
PUNCTUATION NO
READS HEBREW
LEFT TO RIGHT

TEBAHPLA WERBEH EHT
—SRETTEL 22 FO STSISNOC
—STNANOSNOC MEHT FO LLA
SRETTEL ESACREPPU LLA
NOITAUTCNUP ON
SDAER WERBEH
TFEL OT THGIR

Whatdayaknow

		True	False
1	Blessed just means to be financially rich	❏	❏
2	Biblically, "walk" can be defined as "how I behave myself"	❏	❏
3	I decide what and who I follow	❏	❏
4	My course of life, mode of action, road trodden is my choice	❏	❏
5	Sinners are offenders/accounted guilty	❏	❏
6	"Sitting down" with someone can imply judging others	❏	❏
7	If you mock others, you are scornful	❏	❏
8	Whatever you find valuable is what you delight in	❏	❏
9	What I value is something that matters in my mind	❏	❏
10	God's laws are impossible to keep	❏	❏
11	King David wrote all the Psalms	❏	❏
12	The Psalms were written in the Biblical/Classic Hebrew language.	❏	❏
13	The English transliteration of the Hebrew word LORD is Yehovah	❏	❏
14	The letter "J" does not exist in the Hebrew language	❏	❏
15	Eastern meditation is biblical	❏	❏
16	There are two times a Believer should meditate	❏	❏
17	I am accountable for everything I think or do	❏	❏
18	The godly/righteous should be like a tree	❏	❏
19	Believers should have "fruit"	❏	❏
20	I should have a perspective of where I'm going	❏	❏
21	If I am not growing, I might be withering	❏	❏
22	I don't like to think about what happens after death	❏	❏
23	Those who are grounded in God shall prosper	❏	❏
24	Chaff is a valuable part of grain	❏	❏
25	Chaff is heavy/weighty	❏	❏
26	The ungodly will not be judged	❏	❏
27	Sinners will not be in the assemblage of the righteous	❏	❏
28	I am accountable to God	❏	❏
29	The LORD knows the journey I take	❏	❏
30	I am prepared for judgment and eternity	❏	❏
31	The grim alternative to a life of faith in God concerns me	❏	❏
32	My way is preferred over God's	❏	❏
33	It is possible to know what awaits me after death	❏	❏
34	I am ___% **certain** I will go *directly* to heaven when I die	☞	

Pray it Read it Observe it Back it up Express it

Whatdayaknow *(continued)*

Write about any *one or more* of the questions on the previous page. Write until this page is full.

_____

_____

_____

_____

_____

_____

_____

_____

_____

_____

_____

_____

_____

_____

_____

_____

_____

_____

_____

RenewingLives.com

"You can't understand the word of God
unless you understand the words."TM

❏ **Pray it**—Prayer is simply "talking to God" silently in your heart/mind, verbally, or through writing. For Believers, praying should be as common as thinking. There are so many reasons to pray, including your need for wisdom, guidance, strength to resist temptation, and the Holy Spirit's intervention to fight Spiritual battles. Prayer is meant to teach you how to converse with God, recall comfort from His word, and grow in faith as you submit to His will.

There is no special formula, order, or wording needed to pray. Your sincere desire to connect to the Lord in God-honoring honesty, thoughts, and words (seasoned with humility) is the only requirement. Even though God knows your heart, He wants you to communicate your desires, emotions, and needs.

There is no particular way to pray, no special position to pray in, and no limitations on who, what, where, when, why, or how. Your speech or language doesn't need to be different or "religious." Be yourself. Prayer can be a time to support and encourage others, but it should not be used as an opportunity to draw attention to yourself, criticize, fuel gossip, show off, spread rumors, etc.

Jesus gave an example of prayer referred to as "The Lord's Prayer" in Matthew 6:9-13. Although it is always good to memorize scripture for the benefit of yourself and others, God wants intimate communication with you—not a passionless repetition of words He authored. What you mean matters more than what you say. So, pray, talk, and write from your heart.

Ask the LORD to help you set aside the cares of this world as you start your probe into God's word. Begin by "talking to God" in thought, on paper, out loud, or any other way that works for you. Share your concerns. Loving relationships require trust, and that is established by truth.

As you study the Bible, there will be times when your attention is challenged, such as if you worry about someone or something. Use the **Prayer List** to record people and concerns you want to remember to pray for. If you write your concerns down, you will be more likely to continue your study less distracted and with better focus.

Prayer includes:

Adoration noun [the act of paying honors to a divine being, **e.g.,** the true God; the worship of what is due to God; the act of addressing as God; to pay respect to by external action accompanied with the highest reverence; profound (humble/deep) reverence.]

Honor noun [to revere; to respect; to treat with deference (yielding in opinion or judgment), submission and perform relative duties to; to manifest the highest veneration (respect mingled with some degree of awe) for in words and actions; to entertain the most exalted thoughts of; to worship; to adore; to raise to distinction or notice; to elevate in rank or station; to exalt; to glorify; to render illustrious (conspicuous; distinguished by the reputation of greatness; renowned; eminent (exalted in rank; dignified; distinguished.))]

Praise noun and verb transitive [to commend; to applaud; to express approbation (approving/support) of personal worth or actions; to extol (raise) in words or song; to magnify; to glorify on account of perfections or excellent works; to express gratitude for personal favors; to do honor to; to display the excellence of.]

Respect noun and verb transitive [to regard; to have regard to in design or purpose, relation or connection; to view or consider with some degree of reverence; to esteem as possessed of real worth.]

Confession noun [the acknowledgment of a crime, fault or something to one's disadvantage; open declaration of guilt, failure, debt, accusation, etc.; avowal (an open declaration; frank acknowledgment); the act of profession in disclosing sins or faults; the disburdening of the conscience to another.]

Thankfulness noun [expression of gratitude; acknowledgment of a favor; a lively sense of good received; grateful (having a due sense of benefits; kindly disposed towards one from whom a favor has been received); impressed with a sense of kindness received and ready to acknowledge it.]

Supplication noun [to earnestly humbly request God's aid; entreaty (urgent prayer; earnest petition; pressing solicitation); humble, earnest prayer in worship; petition (request).]

Blessing noun [any means of happiness; a gift, benefit or advantage; that which promotes temporal prosperity and welfare or secures everlasting or unlimited felicity (great happiness; blessedness, prosperity; blessing; enjoyment of good.)]

Benefits noun [an act of kindness; a favor conferred (given); advantage; profit; whatever contributes to promote prosperity and personal happiness or add value to property.]

RenewingLives.com

Forgiveness noun *[the act of forgiving, the pardon of an offender by which he is considered and treated as not guilty; the pardon or remission of an offense or crime; disposition to pardon; willingness to forgive; remission of a debt, fine or penalty; to overlook an offense and treat the offender as not guilty.]*

Grace noun *[favor; good will; kindness; the free unmerited love and favor of God as the spring and source of all the benefits men receive from him; favorable influence of God; divine influence or the influence of the spirit in renewing the heart and restraining from sin; the application of Christ's righteousness to the sinner; a state of reconciliation to God; virtuous or religious affection or disposition; faith, meekness, humility, patience, etc., proceeding from divine influence; spiritual instruction, improvement, and edification; eternal life; final salvation; mercy; pardon.]*

Intervention noun *[a state of coming or being between; agency of persons between persons; interposition (intervention) in favor of another; mediation; any interference that may affect the interests of others; a voluntary undertaking of one party for another.]*

Mercy noun *[that benevolence, mildness or tenderness of heart which disposes a person to overlook injuries or to treat an offender better than he deserves; the disposition that tempers justice and induces an injured person to forgive trespasses and injuries and to forbear punishment or inflict less than law or justice will warrant. In this sense, there is perhaps no word in our language precisely synonymous with mercy. That which comes nearest to it is grace. It implies benevolence, tenderness, mildness, pity or compassion, and clemency, but exercised only towards offenders. Mercy is a distinguishing attribute of the Supreme Being; pity; compassion manifested towards a person in distress; clemency and bounty; charity and benevolence; grace; favor; eternal life, the fruit of mercy; pardon; the act of sparing or the forbearance of a violent act expected; to be or to lie at the mercy of, to have no means of self-defense but to be dependent for safety on the mercy or compassion of another, or in the power of that which is irresistible.]*

Peace noun *[a state of quiet or tranquility; freedom from disturbance or agitation; absence of chaos; applicable to society, to individuals, or to the temper of the mind; freedom from war or internal commotion; freedom from private quarrels, suits or disturbance; public quiet; freedom from agitation or disturbance by the passions, as from fear, terror, anger, anxiety or the like; quietness of mind; calmness; quiet of conscience; heavenly rest; the happiness of heaven; harmony; concord (agreement between persons; union in opinions, sentiments, views or interests; peace; harmony); a state of reconciliation between parties at variance; that quiet, order and security which is guaranteed by the laws.]*

Prayer List—[a simple series of the names of persons, objects, numerals, or words]

Date   Person/concern

_____ | _____

_____ | _____

_____ | _____

_____ | _____

_____ | _____

_____ | _____

_____ | _____

_____ | _____

_____ | _____

_____ | _____

_____ | _____

_____ | _____

_____ | _____

_____ | _____

_____ | _____

_____ | _____

_____ | _____

_____ | _____

_____ | _____

_____ | _____

RenewingLives.com

Be anxious for nothing: but in everything by prayer and supplication with thanksgiving let your requests be made known to God. And the peace of God, which passes all understanding, shall keep your hearts and minds through Christ Jesus. Philippians 4:6-7

Pray—Write out a prayer of your heart to "talk to God" including *one or more* of:

❑ **A**doration/honor/praise/respect ❑ **C**onfession ❑ **T**hankfulness ❑ **S**upplication

Supplication means to earnestly and humbly request God's aid in:
❑ **B**lessing/benefits ❑ **F**orgiveness ❑ **G**race ❑ **I**ntervention ❑ **M**ercy ❑ **P**eace

_____

_____

_____

_____

_____

_____

_____

_____

_____

_____

_____

_____

_____

_____

_____

_____

_____

_____

_____

_____

Excerpt from: "123 Pray" (available Online or through your local bookstore).

Bullet Point [used to signify importance; any point worthy of special emphasis.]

- _____
  _____
- _____
  _____
- _____
  _____
- _____
  _____
- _____
  _____
- _____
  _____
- _____
  _____
- _____
  _____
- _____
  _____
- _____
  _____
- _____
  _____
- _____

RenewingLives.com

Pray it—Insight, lists, questions, notes, thoughts, etc.

Read it

"You can't understand the word of God
if you don't understand the words."™

❑ **Read it**—verb *[to inspect, understand, utter, and/or pronounce printed or written words, characters, or symbols in the proper order.]*

The goal of reading the Bible is to:
a) Exercise your mental thinking processes to
b) understand and contain its teaching and ideas *[thoughts, opinions, purposes, intentions or suggestions to possible courses of action]* and
c) nourish a meaningful relationship with the LORD.

When you read, your mind decodes letters to words. Each word has a particular meaning. A body of words used in a particular language is called "vocabulary." It takes vocabulary knowledge to read well, at a good pace, and comprehend *[understand; grasp the meaning; take hold in the mind]* what you have read.

Choose a reading plan from the list below. It might help to log your progress.

A ❑ Read the entire *book* of study in one sitting (without stopping).

B ❑ Read the entire *chapter* of study ❑ 1 ❑ 2 or ❑ 3 times in one sitting.

C ❑ Read the entire chapter of study ❑ 1 ❑ 2 or ❑ 3 times in one day.

D ❑ Read the chapter of study ❑ 1 ❑ 2 or ❑ 3 times *a day* for seven days.

E ❑ Read the chapter *out loud* to ❑ yourself or ❑ another person.

F ❑ Read the chapter to yourself ❑ at your regular pace, or ❑ quickly.

G ❑ Read the chapter to yourself ❑ *slowly* (which is known to reduce stress while deepening your ability to think, concentrate, and absorb information.)

H ❑ Read 1 chapter a day until the entire *book* you are studying is finished.

I ❑ Read __ minutes a day until the entire *book* you are studying is finished.

M ❑ My plan: _____

_____

_____

_____

Psalm 1

Chapter Notes _____

Important Word(s)/Phrase: _____

Vital (Key) Verse: _____

Who—Author/Recipients/Others: _____

What—Subject/Theme/Topic: _____

When—Time/Season: _____

Where—Location: _____

Why—Objective/Purpose: _____

How—Doctrine/Teaching: _____

— _____   — _____

— _____   — _____

— _____   — _____

— _____   — _____

— _____   — _____

— _____   — _____

— _____   — _____

— _____   — _____

— _____   — _____

— _____   — _____

— _____   — _____

— _____   — _____

— _____   — _____

— _____   — _____

— _____   — _____

— _____   — _____

— _____   — _____

— _____   — _____

1

:1 Blessed is the man that walks not in the

counsel of the ungodly, nor stands in the way

of sinners, nor sits in the seat of the scornful.

2 But his delight is in the law of the LORD; and

in his law does he meditate day and night.

3 And he shall be like a tree planted by the

rivers of water, that brings forth his fruit in

his season; his leaf also shall not wither;

and whatsoever he does shall prosper.

4 The ungodly are not so: but are like

the chaff which the wind drives away.

5 Therefore the ungodly shall not stand

in the judgment, nor sinners in the

congregation of the righteous.

6 For the LORD knows the way of the righteous:

but the way of the ungodly shall perish. ■

Read it

PROBE Bible Study – Psalm 1

Read & Rewrite—*[to form characters, letters or figures, as representatives of sounds or ideas; to copy; to transcribe.]*

Read and choose ❏ *one* verse ❏ a few *connected/related* verses to meditate on:

I considered verse(s):_____ then chose:_____

❏ ASV ❏ CSB ❏ ESV ❏ KJV ❏ KJT ❏ NASB ❏ NIV ❏ NKJV ❏ NLT ❏ _____

Hand copy the verse(s) you chose to ponder on the lines that follow.

❏ Use your normal Bible or ❏ a different translation.

❏ Write the verse(s) multiple times or ❏ write from a variety of translations.

❏ Insert a *brief* ❏ regular or ❏ Bible dictionary definition (in parenthesis) following each word you are curious to know its **possible** meaning.

Book: _____ Chapter: _____ Verse(s): _____

_____

_____

_____

_____

_____

_____

_____

_____

_____

_____

_____

_____

_____

_____

_____

_____

_____

Read it

Bullet Points *[used to signify importance; any point worthy of special emphasis.]*

- _____
  _____

- _____
  _____

- _____
  _____

- _____
  _____

- _____
  _____

- _____
  _____

- _____
  _____

- _____
  _____

- _____
  _____

- _____
  _____

- _____
  _____

- _____

RenewingLives.com

Read it—Insight, lists, questions, notes, thoughts, etc.

Observe it

"You can't understand the word of God
unless you understand the words."™

❏ **Observe it**—verb transitive *[to keep or hold in view; keep the eyes on; to see or behold with attention; to take notice; to inspect alongside; to note assiduously (diligently; attentively; with earnestness and care; with regular attendance) or scrupulously (with regard to minute/small particulars and exact propriety/consistency with established principles, rules or customs)]*

At this stage, you'll observe the text *[written words]* and pay attention to sentence structure. All complete sentences include a subject (or doer) and the predicate (or description of what is being done).

Careful observation of the text requires repetitive review. This fact-finding mission trains you to ask questions as basic as "who is doing what?"

From the text, you'll make lists, answer the 5W's & H, and learn to be inquisitive *[inclined to seek knowledge by discussion, investigation, observation, and research.]* Observing the text is the bedrock of Bible study. The purpose of observing the text is to:

1) Discover what you find significant *[anything that supports and conveys meaning; whatever is expressive or representative of events, facts, and principles.].*

2) Catch the sense *[perception, discernment, understanding, reasonable/rational meaning, judgment, consciousness, conviction]* or impression *[effect or image in your heart or mind]* intended by the writer(s).

3) Record details to help seal it in your memory. As you respond to the questions provided, your English grammar *[principles and rules of the written language]* skills will improve from your active involvement in learning.

Note: When you know what God's word teaches, you are less likely to behave in opposition to it.

> **"Your word have I hid in my heart, that I might not sin against you."**
> Psalm 119:11

On the next page, you'll find an example of a "Chapter Notes" page.
❏ Go back to page 28 and jot down what you notice from the chapter.

Proverbs 14

Chapter Notes

Create your own chapter title

Contrasts: The wise seek wisdom—fools mock

Important Word(s)/Phrase: Wise _____

Vital (Key) Verse: 9 Fools make a mock at sin: but... _____ **EXAMPLE**

Who—Author/Recipients/Others: _____

What—Subject/Theme/Topic: _____

When—Time/Season: _____

Where—Location: _____

Why—Objective/Purpose: To give wisdom to the readers

How—Doctrine/Teaching: Instruction to inform the unlearned

O b s e r v e i t

Reference a verse number.   *Record your insight, that of others, or paraphrase.*

1 Wisdom builds up. ←   1 Fools tear down, destroy.

2 The upright respect the Lord.   2 The perverse despise the Lord.

3 Pride and foolishness go together, evidenced by words.

3 Wise words can preserve/rescue you in many situations.

4 If no work is being accomplished, the place is likely clean.

4 Messiness comes when work is done or growth is occurring.

5 Liars do not make faithful witnesses.

6 The critical, cynical, and/or superficial don't find wisdom.

6 Matt 7:7 Ask and it will be given you: seek, and you will find...

6 If you seek to understand wisdom, knowledge will come to you.

7 Get away from foolish people! 7 Words expose the foolish.

8 Carefully consider and understand the way you are heading.

8 The silliness of a stupid fool deceives him/herself and others.

9 Fools mimic, imitate, sneer, and deride. They laugh at others in contempt [hatred: the act of despising; viewing or considering and treating others as destitute of honor, vile and worthless]. A fool mocks, ridicules, or make sport of others. Fools show disdain which springs from their opinion of the worthlessness of others while having a belief in their own superiority or worth. *— Write in one or both columns.*

About the "Who" – The Author

Note anything that reveals the "who" within the and/or chapter.

Author—noun *[to increase or cause to enlarge. The primary sense is one who brings or causes to come forth; one who produces, creates, or brings into being; as, God is the author of the Universe; the beginner, former, or first mover of any thing; hence, the efficient cause of a thing. It is appropriately applied to one who composes or writes a book or original work.]*

"**All scripture is given by inspiration of God, and is profitable for doctrine, for reproof, for correction, for instruction in righteousness: That the man of God may be perfect, thoroughly furnished unto all good works.**" 2 Timothy 3:16

Inspired and guided by God, man took "pen in hand" to physically record God's message to mankind. We call the writers of the books of the Bible: authors. Look for details you can discover about the author of the book or chapter you are studying in addition to his/her name (if it is revealed.) You'll want to watch for personal pronouns *[a word used to replace a proper noun or a group of people or things to prevent the repetition of it]* such as: he, her, him, I, it, me, she, them, they, us, we, you.

"Who"—pronoun *[refers to persons (who/whom/whose).]*

Use words directly from the text/verse or summarize *[reduce what you discover to a few brief/concise words]* the information. Record the chapter and verse number in the space provided.

C/V#   About the "who"—the author

_____ | _____

_____ | _____

_____ | _____

_____ | _____

_____ | _____

_____ | _____

Observe it

About the "Who" – Subject/Doer & Others

Subject/Doer—noun *[the subject is a grammatical term used to describe the nouns, pronouns, and noun phrases that occur before the verb in a sentence. The subject usually indicates the doer of an action.]*

& Others—noun *[significant people in the passages you are studying.}*
Discover all you can of the people mentioned in the chapter/verse.

Use words directly from the text/verse or summarize *[reduce what you discover to a few brief/concise words]* the information. Record the chapter and verse number in the space provided.

C/V#   S/D=Subject/Doer, O=Others

_____ | ❑ S/D ❑ O _____

_____

_____ | ❑ S/D ❑ O _____

_____

_____ | ❑ S/D ❑ O _____

_____

_____ | ❑ S/D ❑ O _____

_____

_____ | ❑ S/D ❑ O _____

_____

_____ | ❑ S/D ❑ O _____

_____

_____ | ❑ S/D ❑ O _____

_____

_____ | ❑ S/D ❑ O _____

_____

O b s e r v e   i t

RenewingLives.com

About the "What" – Subject/Theme/Topic

Note anything that reveals the "what" of the book and/or chapter.

Subject—noun *[the person or thing discussed, described, or dealt with; the matter or topic presented for consideration in a debate, discussion, thought, or study.]*

Theme—noun *[the chief, main or principal idea, message, subject, or topic a person tries to convey.]*

Topic—noun *[any idea, issue, or subject of argument or discourse (a communication of thoughts by words); In rhetoric, a probable argument drawn from the several circumstances and places of a fact. Note: Rhetoric is the art of speaking with propriety, elegance, and force or the power of persuasion or attraction, which allures or charms.]*

"What"—adjective *[used to inquire of the identity, nature or value of an object, person, or matter; specifies form or manner; a way of acting or being, class or order, rank, condition or quality; distinct particulars.]*

To discover the main theme of a verse, chapter, or book, look for repeated words or phrases that might help expose the topic(s) covered.

Use words directly from the text/verse or summarize *[reduce what you discover to a few brief/concise words]* the information. Record the chapter and verse number in the space provided.

Observe it

Important Repeated words

- _____
- _____
- _____
- _____
- _____
- _____
- _____
- _____
- _____

C/V# About the "what"—subject/theme/topic

____ | _____

_____

_____

_____

____ | _____

_____

_____

_____

About the "When" – Times & Seasons

Note anything that reveals the "where" within the book and/or chapter.

Times *[a particular portion or part of duration, whether past, present, or future; A space or measured portion of duration; the state of things at a particular period.]*

& Seasons *[season literally signifies that which comes or arrives and in this general sense is synonymous with time; one of the four divisions of the year, spring, summer, autumn, winter.]*

Some of the words that *might* indicate time: *after, afterward(s), as soon as, at that time, late, now, soon, then, until, when, while.*

Use words directly from the text/verse or summarize *[reduce what you discover to a few brief/concise words]* the information. Record the chapter and verse number in the space provided.

C/V#   Times & Seasons

_____ | _____

_____ | _____

_____ | _____

_____ | _____

_____ | _____

_____ | _____

_____ | _____

_____ | _____

RenewingLives.com

About the "Where" – Location/Place

Note anything that reveals the "where" within the book and/or chapter.

Location—noun *[a particular place or position; a place of activity, residence, etc.]*

"Where"—adverb *[at, in, or to which place or situation.]*

Some of the words that *might* indicate location: *at, in, on, over, where, wherever.*

Use words directly from the text/verse or summarize *[reduce what you discover to a few brief/concise words]* the information. Record the chapter and verse number in the space provided.

C/V#   Location/Place

_____ | _____

_____ | _____

_____ | _____

_____ | _____

_____ | _____

_____ | _____

_____ | _____

_____ | _____

_____ | _____

Observe it

About the "Why" – Objective/Purpose

Note anything that reveals the "why" of the book and/or chapter.

Objective—noun *[the aim, goal, or end of action; something toward which effort is directed; a thing aimed at or sought.]*

Purpose—noun *[intention, proposal, pursuit; to intend, design, resolve, or determine some end or object to be reached or accomplished; the end or aim to which the view is directed in any plan, measure or exertion; the reason for which something is done, created, created for, made or used; one's aim, desired result, determination, end, goal, objective, or resolve constant in pursuing and to be attained; the reason for which something exists.]*

"Why"—adverb *[for what cause, purpose, or reason.]*

Some of the words that **might** indicate: *so that, in order that, in order to.*

Use words directly from the text/verse or summarize *[reduce what you discover to a few brief/concise words]* the information. Record the chapter and verse number in the space provided.

C/V#   *About the "why"—objective/purpose*

_____ | _____

_____ | _____

_____ | _____

_____ | _____

_____ | _____

_____ | _____

_____ | _____

About the "How" – Doctrine/Teaching

Note anything that reveals the "how" of the book and/or chapter.

Doctrine—noun *[in a general sense, whatever is taught, hence a principle or position in any science; something that is taught; the act of teaching as in Mark 4:2; learning; knowledge as in Isaiah 28:9; the truths of the gospel in general; whatever is laid down as true by an instructor or master, hence a doctrine may be true, false, a mere tenet, or opinion.]*

"How"—adverb *[in what manner, means or way; to what degree or extent; or used to ask about the condition or quality of something.]*

Teaching—noun *[the act or business of instructing to inform the mind; to educate; to impart knowledge to one who was destitute of it.]*

Use words directly from the text/verse or summarize *[reduce what you discover to a few brief/concise words]* the information. Record the chapter and verse number in the space provided.

C/V#   *About the "how"—doctrine/teaching*

_____ | _____

_____

_____

_____ | _____

_____

_____

_____ | _____

_____

_____

_____

O b s e r v e   i t

☞

About the Author's "How" – Doctrine/Teaching *(continued)*

C/V#   *About the "how"—doctrine/teaching*

About Other Observations in the Bible

Cause/Reason—noun *[that which moves the mind to action, phenomenon/ anything observed to exist or happen, or condition; that which by its agency or operation produces what did not before exist.]*
Causes *might* be introduced by the words: *because, for this reason, since, that.*

Comparison—noun *[shows how things are alike by considering the relation between them to discover a) their agreement and resemblance, or b) their disagreement and difference.]*

Comparisons *might* be introduced by the words: allegory, *as, also, better, compare, compared, just as, like, liken, likewise, more, more than, resemble, so as, so also, song, too,* **or** *be one of the parables or proverbs.*

Conclusion—noun *[a termination; conclusion, end; close; the last part; the close of an argument, debate or reasoning; inference that ends the discussion; final decision or result; determination; that which is collected or drawn from premises, propositions, facts, experience, or reasoning; gathers up summarily what has already been said.]*

Conclusions *might* be introduced by the words: *accordingly, finally, for this reason, now therefore, then, these things being so, so, so then, therefore, wherefore.*

Condition—noun *[terms of a contract or covenant; stipulation; that is, that which is set, fixed, established or proposed; that which is established, or to be done, or to happen, as requisite to another act, such as If/Then statements; made with limitations; not absolute; made or granted on certain terms.]*
Conditions *might* be introduced by the word: *as, if/then.*

Continuation—noun *[extension or carrying on to a further point.]*
Continuations *might* be introduced by the words: *and, either, neither, nor, or.*

Contrast—noun *[shows differences, unlikeness, or opposition of things in order to exhibit the superior excellence of one by the inferiority or defects of the other; e.g., "light vs. darkness."]*
Contrasts *might* be introduced with the words: *although, as, but, but rather, despite, even though, however, in theory, in practice, in spite of, like, instead of, nevertheless, nonetheless, on the other hand, rather, spite, unlike, while, whereas, yet.*

Observe it

About Other Observations in the Bible (continued)

Emphasis—noun *[a particular stress of utterance, or force of voice, given to the words or parts of a discourse, whose signification the speaker intends to impress specially upon his audience; or a distinctive utterance of words, specially significant, with a degree and kind of stress suited to convey their meaning in the best manner.]* Conclusions **might** be introduced by the words: *indeed, only.*

Explanation—noun *[the act of explaining, expounding, or interpreting; exposition; illustration; interpretation; the act of clearing from obscurity and making intelligible.]* Conclusions **might** be introduced by the words: *because, for, now.*

Use words directly from the text/verse or summarize *[reduce what you discover to a few brief/concise words]* the information. Record the chapter and verse number in the space provided.

C/V#   **Cr**=Cause/Reason, **Cm**=Comparison, **Cn**=Conclusion, **Cd**=Condition, **Ct**=Continuation, **Co**=Contrast, **Em**=Emphasis, **Ex**=Explanation.

_____ ❑ Cr ❑ Cm ❑ Cn ❑ Cd ❑ Ct ❑ Co ❑ Em ❑ Ex _____

_____

_____

_____ ❑ Cr ❑ Cm ❑ Cn ❑ Cd ❑ Ct ❑ Co ❑ Em ❑ Ex _____

_____

_____

_____ ❑ Cr ❑ Cm ❑ Cn ❑ Cd ❑ Ct ❑ Co ❑ Em ❑ Ex _____

_____

_____ ❑ Cr ❑ Cm ❑ Cn ❑ Cd ❑ Ct ❑ Co ❑ Em ❑ Ex _____

_____

_____

Chapter Outline noun *[general summary of essential points]*

V#'s	Summary

Observe it

❑ Gospel ❑ History ❑ Poetry ❑ Prophecy ❑ Prophets ❑ Law ❑ Letters-Paul ❑ Letters-Leaders

Chapter Summary *[a short account of the main facts or ideas of a larger work]*

Book: _____ Chapter: _____

The three most important repeated words/phrases in the *chapter* are:

1 _____

2 _____

3 _____

The subject matter/theme/topic mentioned most in the *chapter* is:

_____

_____

The discourse/doctrine/teaching mentioned most in the *chapter* is:

_____

_____

The most difficult verse to understand in the *chapter* is:

_____

_____

Create a title for the *chapter* using six (or fewer) words *in your own style*:

_____

_____

Create a title for the *chapter* using six (or fewer) *words found in the text*:

_____

_____

The most vital *[essential, important, necessary]* verse in the *chapter*: _____

_____

_____

Reduce the *chapter* to *three or fewer* words: _____

O b s e r v e   i t

RenewingLives.com

Hebrew Poetry in the Bible

Poetry effectively crafts words into imagery, unlike popular English poetry that tends to be sound-based. Hebrew poetry is often thought-based. Many Psalms are written in a poetic form in which one line corresponds to the other in some way. That style is known as parallelism. Hebrew parallelism uses restatement or repetition of a same or similar idea, meaning, phrase, thought, or word, as well as comparisons *[considers the relation between persons or things]* and contrasts *[identifies differences or opposites]*.

Some of the types of poetic parallelism used in the Bible are:

❏ **Antithetic** (an-tih-THEH-tik) **Parallelism** contrasts the first portion from the second through a restatement of the same idea; the one line presents the opposite of the other:

For the Lord knows <u>the way of the righteous</u>.
But <u>the way of the wicked</u> will perish. Psalm 1:6

❏ **Climactic** (klie-MAK-tik) **Parallelism** uses repetition where the first line is repeated in the next line, and something is added to develop the meaning and complete the sense.

<u>Sing to the Lord</u> a new song;
<u>Sing to the Lord</u>, all the earth.
<u>Sing to the Lord</u>, bless His name; Psalm 96:1-2a

❏ **Emblematic** (em-bleh-MAHH-tik) **Parallelism** uses comparisons where one part is figurative, and the other literal, to form a simile usually with the word "like" or "as"; one line is a simile of the thought in the other line.

<u>As the hart pants</u> after the water brooks,
<u>so pants my soul</u> after you, O God. Psalm 42:1

❏ **Numerical** (new-MER-rih-kl) **Parallelism** states a number then adds an example, quantity, or something more than was previously stated.

Thus says the LORD, "For <u>three</u> transgressions of Israel and for <u>four</u>..." Amos 2:6a

Hebrew Poetry in the Bible *(continued)*

❑ **Synonymous** (sih-NAH-nuh-muhs) **Parallelism** uses repetition without adding or subtracting clarification or anything significant; basically repeats the thought of the first line in different words:

Deliver my soul, O Lord, from lying lips, and
from a deceitful tongue. Psalm 120:2

❑ **Synthetic** (sin-THEH-tik) **Parallelism** occurs when the second portion or idea completes, advances, or develops what was stated in the first by adding clarification.

O come, let us worship and bow down:
let us kneel before the Lord our maker. Psalm 95:6

Observe it

C/V# ***A****=Antithetic,* ***C****=Climactic,* ***E****=Emblematic,* ***N****=Numerical,* ***So****=Synonymous,* ***St****=Synthetic*

____ | ❑ A ❑ C ❑ E ❑ N ❑ So ❑ St __________

____ | ❑ A ❑ C ❑ E ❑ N ❑ So ❑ St __________

____ | ❑ A ❑ C ❑ E ❑ N ❑ So ❑ St __________

____ | ❑ A ❑ C ❑ E ❑ N ❑ So ❑ St __________

____ | ❑ A ❑ C ❑ E ❑ N ❑ So ❑ St __________

Notes on Theology —noun *[the science which teaches the existence, character, and attributes of God, his laws and government, the doctrines we are to believe, and the duties we are to practice. Natural theology is the knowledge we have of God from his works, by the light of nature and reason.]*

Record what you discover about God and any insight you gain.

C/V#   Notes

_____ | _____

_____

_____

_____ | _____

_____

_____

_____ | _____

_____

_____

_____ | _____

_____

_____

_____ | _____

_____

_____

_____ | _____

_____

_____

_____ | _____

_____

Observe it

☞

Notes on Theology *(continued)*

C/V#   Notes

PROBE Bible Study – Psalm 1

Observe it

RenewingLives.com

Repeated words A to Z

Beginning at verse 1, list every single word other than Articles (a, an, the). Use a slash mark to count multiples of the same word, **e.g.,** I=1, II=2, III=3, IIII=4, IIII=5. The results will help you realize repeated words which might be helpful in analyzing the text for English grammar (figures/ parts of speech, literary devices, tenses) and Hebrew poetry types.

A _____ **B** _____ **C** _____ **D** _____ **E** _____ **F** _____

_____ _____ _____ _____ _____ _____

_____ _____ _____ _____ _____ _____

_____ _____ _____ _____ _____ _____

_____ _____ _____ _____ _____ _____

_____ _____ _____ _____ _____ _____

_____ _____ _____ _____ _____ _____

_____ _____ _____ _____ _____ _____

_____ _____ _____ _____ _____ _____

_____ _____ _____ _____ _____ _____

G _____ **H** _____ **I** _____ **J** _____ **K** _____ **L** _____

_____ _____ _____ _____ _____ _____

_____ _____ _____ _____ _____ _____

_____ _____ _____ _____ _____ _____

_____ _____ _____ _____ _____ _____

_____ _____ _____ _____ _____ _____

_____ _____ _____ _____ _____ _____

_____ _____ _____ _____ _____ _____

_____ _____ _____ _____ _____ _____

Observe it

Repeated words A to Z *(continued)*

M_____ N _____ O _____ P _____ Q_____ R _____

_____ _____ _____ _____ _____ _____

_____ _____ _____ _____ _____ _____

_____ _____ _____ _____ _____ _____

_____ _____ _____ _____ _____ _____

_____ _____ _____ _____ _____ _____

_____ _____ _____ _____ _____ _____

_____ _____ _____ _____ _____ _____

O b s e r v e   i t

S_____ T _____ U _____ V _____ W_____ X _____

_____ _____ _____ _____ _____ _____

_____ _____ _____ _____ _____ _____

_____ _____ _____ _____ _____ _____

_____ _____ _____ _____ _____ _____

_____ _____ _____ _____ _____ _____

_____ _____ _____ _____ _____ _____

_____ _____ _____ _____ _____ _____

Y _____ _____ Z _____

_____ _____ _____

_____ _____ _____

RenewingLives.com

Post-in' Notes & Quotes

Bullet Points *[used to signify importance; any point worthy of special emphasis.]*

- _____
- _____
- _____
- _____
- _____
- _____
- _____
- _____
- _____
- _____
- _____
- _____

Observe it

RenewingLives.com

Observe it—Insight, lists, questions, notes, thoughts, etc.

Back it up

"You can't understand the word of God
if you don't understand the words."™

❏ 𝕭ack-it-up—

"Study to show yourself approved to God, a workman that needs not to be ashamed, rightly dividing the word of truth." 2 Timothy 2:15

The English idiom *[an expression peculiar from the common manner of speaking]* **"back it up"** means demonstrating or proving by facts something to be true.

In this fourth step, you'll use details noticed from observation in an "epic" *[extending beyond the usual or ordinary, especially in size or scope]* study of God's word (**E**xamine, **P**rove, **I**nterpret, **C**ompose).

a) **Examine** *[inquire into circumstances, facts, and truth=the real state of a thing]*...

...Through **inquiry** *[search for truth, information, or knowledge; research; examination into facts or principles by proposing and discussing questions]*.

...Through **resources** to study, weigh, and compare facts, i.e., ancient maps, Bible commentaries, concordances, cross-references, dictionaries, encyclopedias, historical documents, interlinear Bibles, lectures, lexicons, teachings, etc.

b) **Prove** *[to make certain fact, truth, or reality by argument, induction, reasoning, testimony, or other evidence]*...

...By **argument** *[a reason offered in proof to induce belief or convince the mind followed by for or against; in logic, an inference drawn from premises, which are indisputable, or at least of probable truth]*.

...By **evidence** *[that which makes clear and enables the mind to apprehend truth; or in a manner to convince it]*.

...By **reasoning** *[that act or operation of the mind by which new or unknown propositions are deduced from previous known and evident, or which are admitted or supposed for the sake of argument]*.

...By **testimony** *[a solemn declaration or affirmation made to establish or prove some fact]*.

c) **Interpret** *[separate one thing from another; understand the differences and judge the meaning of information, words, or actions]*. The art of expounding the Scriptures comes from interpreting, explaining, and unfolding the signification, known as *hermeneutics*. To interpret...

...Analyze without **bias** *[that which causes the mind to lean or incline from a state of indifference to a particular course, object, or prejudice]*.

...Determine the **Literary** *[written composition]* **type:** ❏ Gospel ❏ History ❏ Poetry ❏ Prophecy ❏ Prophets ❏ Law ❏ Letters-Paul ❏ Letters-Leaders. The writing style in the books of the law will be quite different from poetry. Proverbs of general truths differ from parables, and so on.

...Ignore **punctuation** *[dividing writing into sentences and clauses, or the addition of a period (.); colon (:); semicolon (;); comma (,), etc. Original Hebrew scrolls did not designate paragraphs nor contain punctuation. Scholars later added paragraphs and punctuation.*

...Keep in **context** *[the passages of scripture which are near the text, either before it or after it. The sense of a passage of scripture is often illustrated by the context]*. Consider the *nearby context* (words, phrases, or sentences immediately before or after) as well as the *overall context* (paragraphs and chapters). Errors in interpretation occur when passages are taken out of context, isolated without consideration of context, or a combination of the nearby and overall context is ignored.

...Let **scripture interpret** scripture *[what is written in the Old and New Testament]*. Cross-reference other passages in the Bible to what you are studying. A word or phrase found in a separate verse will not necessarily be from the same Aramaic, Greek, or Hebrew root word.

...Pay attention to **repetition** *[in rhetoric, repeating the same word, or the same sense in different words, to make a deeper impression on the audience]*. Repeated words and phrases might emphasize importance.

...Understand **customs** *[frequent or common use, or practice; a frequent repetition of the same act or way; an established manner; habitual practice]*. The word "culture" does not appear in the Bible. Modern-day usage refers to the whole of a people group and their way of life, including attire, beliefs, habits, knowledge, laws, morals, rituals, social norms, etc.

...Understand **definitions** *[an explanation of the signification of a word or term, or what a word is meant to express]* of words. Words express God's ideas, His divine revelation, or the thoughts in the mind of mankind. Sometimes words are inadequate in accomplishing a clear

RenewingLives.com

understanding of what was intended in the original Aramaic, Greek, or Hebrew language.

…Understand **etymology** [*That part of philology (a love of words and desire to know the origin and construction of language) which explains the origin and derivation of words, to ascertain their radical or primary signification; in grammar, etymology comprehends the various inflections and modifications of words, and shows how they were formed from their simple roots*].

…Understand **figures of speech** [*in grammar, any deviation from the rules of analogy or syntax; in rhetoric, a mode of speaking or writing in which words are deflected from their ordinary signification, or a manner more beautiful, forceful, impressive, or strong than the ordinary way of expressing the sense*]. E.W. Bullinger notes there are two-hundred-seventeen (217) figures of speech, many of which are in the Bible.

…Understand **history** [*an account of facts, particularly of facts respecting nations or states; a narration of events in the order in which they happened, with their causes and effects*]. Historical accounts and timelines are necessary for understanding the Bible.

d) **Compose** your judgment or opinion…

…Put together a reasonable defense of your **judgment** [*the determination of the mind formed from comparing the relations of ideas, or the comparison of facts and arguments to ascertain truth*] or **opinion** [*the decision the mind forms of truth or falsehood (which is supported by a degree of evidence that renders it probable but does not produce absolute knowledge or certainty)*].

> **"But sanctify the Lord God in your hearts:
> <u>and be ready always to give an answer</u> to every man
> that asks you a reason of the hope that is in you
> with meekness and fear:"** 1 Peter 3:15

M. Henry's Commentary —noun *[comments, expositions, explanations, or illustrations of difficult and obscure passages; a book of comments or annotations.]*

RenewingLives.com

Matthew Henry (October 18, 1662—June 22, 1714)

Matthew Henry was a non-conformist minister (a Protestant/Christian who did not conform to the government, authority, or control of the Church of England). He was also an author, preacher, and scholar. He began reading and writing Greek and Latin by age nine, then added to his learning Hebrew and French. At age 25, he married. Two years later, his wife died of smallpox shortly after childbirth then his only child died. He remarried but suffered the loss of his second and third child in infancy. All total, he had nine children. He endured difficult health issues from childhood until his death.

Matthew Henry was a gifted speaker. He traveled extensively to teach the Bible. His approach to teaching was *"Choose for your pulpit subjects the plainest, and most needful truths, and endeavor to make them plainer."*

He is best known for his six-volume biblical commentary *"Exposition of the Old and New Testaments"* (1706) in which he gave an exhaustive account of every verse in the Bible. His commentaries are the most widely used of its kind.

The following are examples of Matthew Henry's insight:

"We should take heed of pride; it is a sin that turned angels into devils."

"The Bible is a letter God has sent to us; prayer is a letter we send to him."

"Hope for the best, get ready for the worst, and then take what God chooses to send."

"Everlasting life is a jewel of too great a value to be purchased by the wealth of this world."

"It ought to be the business of every day to prepare for our last day."

"God has wisely kept us in the dark concerning future events and reserved for himself the knowledge of them, that he may train us up in a dependence upon himself and a continued readiness for every event."

"Christ's followers cannot expect better treatment in the world than their Master had."

Back it up

Commentaries assist in the understanding of difficult and obscure *[not easily understood, what is not obvious]* passages *[parts of a book or writing]* including:

Annotations *[notes, remarks, and comments intended to illustrate the meaning of a passage of scripture]*;

Explanations *[make plain or intelligible, expound to clear from obscurity; interpret to unfold the meaning of anything not understood such as: enigmas/obscure sayings with hidden meanings, dreams, predictions, visions]*;

Expositions *[expose to give an unobstructed view to the sense or meaning of the author or writing]*;

Illustrations *[elucidation to explain and make clear what is obscure or abstruse/concealed, hidden, or difficult to be comprehended or understood; opposed to what is obvious.]*

B a c k   i t   u p

Note: Archibald Alexander, D.D. (Doctor of Divinity) and Reverend Edward Bickersteth provided prefatory remarks in Matthew Henry's commentary. Both were influential in his learning and life.

*The original 1706 version is updated as follows: Antiquated words and spellings appear in contemporary English. The text is large print in a visually consistent format. Webster's 1828 definitions are inserted in brackets [ ] to improve clarity and increase understanding. The 1611 King James Version (KJV) is converted to King James Today (KJT).

An Exposition with Practical Observations of the Book of Psalms*
Matthew Henry (1706)

The Book of Psalms

Introduction

We have now before us one of the choicest and most excellent parts of all the Old Testament; nay *[not only so]*, so much is there in it of Christ and his gospel *[good or joyful message]*, as well as of God and his law, that it had been called the abstract *[separate; distinct]*, or summary, of both Testaments. The History of Israel, which we were long upon, let us to camps and council-boards, and there entertained *[kept, held or maintained in the mind with favor]* and instructed us in the knowledge of God. The book of Job brought us into the schools, and treated us with profitable disputations *[a reasoning or argumentation in opposition to something]* concerning God and his providence *[foresight accompanied with the procurement of what is necessary for future use]*. But this book brings us into the sanctuary *[a house consecrated to the worship of God]*, draws us off from converse *[mutual communication of thoughts and opinions]* with men, with the politicians, philosophers, or disputers of this world, and directs us into communion *[fellowship]* with God, by solacing *[relieving grief; cheering in affliction]* and reposing *[laying at rest; placing in confidence]* our souls in him, lifting up and letting out our hearts towards him. Thus may we be in the mount with God; and we understand not our interests if we say not, It is good to be here. Let us consider,

I. The title of this book. It is called,

1. The Psalms; under that title it is referred to, Luke 24:44. The Hebrew calls it Tehillim, which properly signifies Psalms of praise, because many of them are such; but Psalms is a more general word, meaning all metrical

compositions fitted to be sung, which may as well be historical, doctrinal *[something taught]*, or supplicatory, as laudatory *[containing praise]*. Though singing be properly the voice of joy, yet the intention of songs is of a much greater latitude *[extent]*, to assist the memory, and both to express and to excite all the other affections as well as this of joy. The priests had a mournful muse *[deep thought]* as well as joyful ones; and the divine institution of singing psalms is thus largely intended; for we are directed not only to praise God, but to teach and admonish ourselves and one another in psalms, and hymns, and spiritual songs, **Colossians 3:16.**

2. It is called the Book of Psalms; so it is quoted by St. Peter, **Acts 1:20.** It is a collection of psalms, of all the psalms that were divinely *[by the agency or influence of God]* inspired, which, though composed at several times and upon several occasions, are here put together without any reference to or dependence upon one another; thus they were preserved from being scattered and lost, and were in so much greater readiness for the service of the church. See what a good master we serve, and what pleasantness there is in wisdom's ways, when we are not only commanded to sing at our work, and have cause enough given us to do so, but have words also put in our mouths and songs prepared to our hands.

II. The author of this book. It is, no doubt, derived originally from the blessed Spirit. They are spiritual songs, words which the Holy Ghost taught. The penman of most of them was David the son of Jesse, who is therefore called the sweet psalmist of Israel, **2 Samuel 23:1.** Some that have not his name in their titles yet are expressly ascribed to him elsewhere, as **Psalm 2** (**Acts 4:25**) and **Psalm 96** and **105** (**1 Chronicles 16**). One psalm is expressly said to be the prayer of Moses (**Psalm 90**); and that some of the psalms were penned by Asaph is intimated *[hinted; slightly mentioned or signified]*, **2 Chronicles 29:30**, where they are said to praise the Lord in the words of David and Asaph, who is there called a seer *[a person who forsees future events]* or prophet. Some of the psalms seem to have been penned long after, as **Psalm 137**, at the time of the captivity in Babylon; but the far greater part of them were certainly penned by David himself, whose genius *[uncommon powers of intellect]* lay towards poetry and music, and who was raised up, qualified, and animated *[lively; full of spirit]*, for the establishing of the ordinance *[rule established by authority]* of singing psalms in the church of God,

**B
a
c
k

i
t

u
p**

as Moses and Aaron were, in their day, for the settling of the ordinances of sacrifice; theirs is superseded *[made void; suspended]*, but his remains, and will to the end of time, when it shall be swallowed up in the songs of eternity. Herein David was a type of Christ, who descended from him, not from Moses, because he came to take away sacrifice (the family of Moses was soon lost and extinct), but to establish and perpetuate *[to be continued indefinitely]* joy and praise; for of the family of David in Christ there shall be no end.

III. The scope of it. It is manifestly intended,

1. To assist the exercises of natural religion, and to kindle in the souls of men those devout *[devoted]* affections which we owe to God as our Creator, owner, ruler, and benefactor. The book of Job helps to prove our first principles of the divine *[pertaining to the true God]* perfections and providence; but this helps to improve them in prayers and praises, and professions of desire towards him, dependence on him, and an entire devotedness and resignation *[submission]* to him. Other parts of scripture show that God is infinitely above man, and his sovereign *[supreme in power and dominion]* Lord; but this shows us that he may, notwithstanding *[not opposing]*, be conversed with by us sinful worms of the earth; and there are ways in which, if it be not our own fault, we may keep up communion *[fellowship]* with him in all the various conditions of human life.

2. To advance the excellencies of revealed *[made known]* religion, and in the most pleasing powerful manner to recommend it to the world. There is indeed little or nothing of the ceremonial law in all the book of Psalms. Though sacrifice and offering were yet to continue many ages, yet they are here represented as things which God did not desire (**Psalm 40:6, 51:16**), as things comparatively little, and which in time were to vanish away. But the word and law of God, those parts of it which are moral *[relating to the practice, manners or conduct of men as social beings in relation to each other, and with reference to right and wrong]* and of perpetual *[never ceasing]* obligation are here all along magnified and made honorable, nowhere more. And Christ, the crown and center of revealed religion, the foundation, corner, and top-stone, of that blessed building, is here clearly spoken of in type *[a figure of something to come]* and prophecy *[a declaration of something to come]*, his sufferings and the glory *[brightness; luster; splendor]* that should follow, and the kingdom that he should set up in the world, in which God's covenant *[the commands, prohibitions, and promises of God]* with David, concerning his kingdom, was to have its accomplishment. What a high value does this book put upon the word of God, his statutes *[commandments; decrees; ordinances]* and judgments, his covenant and the great and precious promises of it; and how does it recommend them to us as our guide and stay, and our heritage for ever!

IV. The use of it. All scripture, being given by inspiration of God, is profitable to convey divine light into our understandings; but this book is of singular use with that to convey *[carry; transmit]* divine life and power, and a holy warmth, into our affections. There is no one book of scripture that is more helpful to the devotions of the saints than this, and it has been so in all ages of the church, ever since it was written and the several parts of it were delivered to the chief musician for the service of the church.

1. It is of use to be sung. Further than David's psalms we may go, but we need not, for hymns *[ode in honor of God]* and spiritual songs. What the rules of the Hebrew meter *[measure; verse; arrangement of poetical feet or of long and short syllables in verse]* were even the learned are not certain. But these psalms ought to be rendered *[assigned; translated]* according to the meter of every language, at least so as that they may be sung for the edification *[building up]* of the church. And I think it is a great comfort to us, when we are singing David's psalms, that we are offering the very same praises to God that were offered to him in the days of David and the other godly kings of Judah. So rich, so well made, are these divine poems, that they can never be exhausted, can never be worn thread-bare.

2. It is of use to be read and opened by the ministers *[chief servants]* of Christ, as containing great and excellent truths, and rules concerning good and evil. Our Lord Jesus expounded the psalms to his disciples, the gospel psalms, and opened their understandings (for he had the key of David) to understand them, **Luke 24:44**.

3. It is of use to be read and meditated *[dwelled on in thought]* upon by all good people. It is a full fountain, out of which we may all be drawing water with joy.

(1.) The Psalmist's experiences are of great use for our direction, caution, and encouragement. In telling us, as he often does, what passed between God and his soul, he lets us know what we may expect from God, and what he will expect, and require, and graciously accept, from us. David was a man after God's own heart, and therefore those who find themselves in some measure *[extent]* according to his heart have reason to hope that they are renewed *[made new again; revived]* by the grace of God, after the image of God, and many have much comfort in the testimony of their consciences *[moral sense; internal self-knowledge]* for them that they can heartily say Amen to David's prayers and praises.

(2.) Even the Psalmist's expressions too are of great use; and by them the Spirit helps our praying infirmities *[weakness]*, because we know not what to pray for as we ought. In all our approaches to God, as well as in our first returns to God, we are directed to take with us words (**Hosea 14:2**), these word, words which the Holy Ghost *[the third person in the Trinity (the union of three persons in one Godhead, the Father, the Son, and the Holy Spirit)]* teaches. If we make David's psalms familiar to us, as we ought to do, whatever errand *[special business]* we have at the throne of grace, by way of confession *[the acknowledgment of a crime, fault; open declaration of guilt, failure, debt, accusation, etc.]*, petition *[a request for something needed or desired]*, or thanksgiving *[expressing gratitude for favors or mercies]*, we may thence *[from that place]* be assisted in the delivery of it; whatever devout *[devoted]* affection is working in us, holy desire or hope, sorrow or joy, we may there find apt *[fit; suitable]* words wherewith *[with which]* to clothe it, sound speech which cannot be condemned *[pronounced to be wrong, guilty, worthless or forfeited]*. It will be good to collect the most proper and lively expressions of devotion which we find here, and to methodize *[arrange in a convenient manner]* them, and reduce them to the several heads *[chief; principle]* of prayer, that they may be the more ready to us. Or we may take sometimes one choice psalm and sometimes another, and pray it over, that is, enlarge upon each verse in our own thoughts, and offer up our meditations to God as they arise from the expressions we find there. The learned Dr. Hammond, in his preface to his paraphrase on the Psalms (Section 29), says, "That going over a few psalms with these interpunctions *[the making of points between sentences or parts of a sentence]* of mental devotion, suggested, animated, and maintained, by the native life and vigor which is in the psalms, is much to be preferred before the saying over the whole Psalter *[book of Psalms]*, since nothing is more fit to be averted *[to turn from]* in religious offices than their degenerating into heartless dispirited recitations.' If, as St. Austin advises, we form our spirit by the affection of the psalm, we may then be sure of acceptance with God in using the language of it. Nor is it only our devotion, and the affections of our mind, that the book of Psalms assists, teaching us how to offer praise so as to glorify God, but, it is also a directory to the actions of our lives, and teaches us how to order our conversation aright *[rightly; without mistake or crime]*, so as that, in the end, we may see the salvation of God, **Psalm 50:23**. The Psalms were thus serviceable to the Old-Testament church, but to us Christians they may be of more use than they could be to those who lived before the coming of Christ; for, as Moses's sacrifices, so David's songs, are expounded *[explained; laid open; interpreted]* and made more intelligible *[understood]* by the gospel of Christ, which lets us within the veil; so that if to David's prayers and praises we add St. Paul's prayers in his epistles, and the new songs in the Revelation, we shall be thoroughly furnished for this good work; for the scripture, perfected, makes the man of God perfect.

As to the division of this book, we need not be solicitous *[anxious; concerned]*; there is no connexion *[connection]* (or very seldom) between one psalm and another, nor any reason discernible *[that may be seen distinctly; distinguishable]* for the placing of them in the order wherein *[in which]* we here find them; but it seems to be ancient, for that which is now the second psalm was so in the apostles' time, **Acts 13:33**. The common Latin joins the **9th** and **10th** together; all popish authors quote by that, so that, thenceforward *[from that time onward]*, throughout the book, their number is one short of ours; our **11** is their **10**, our **119** is their **118**. But they divide the **147th** into two, and so make up the number of **150**. Some have endeavored *[exerted intellectual or physical power]* to reduce the psalms to proper heads, according to the matter of them, but there is often such a variety of matter in one and the same psalm that this cannot be done with any certainty. But the seven penitential *[expressing penitence or contrition of heart]* Psalms have been in a particular manner singled out by the devotions of many. They are reckoned to be **Psalm 6, 32, 38, 51, 102, 130**, and **143**. The Psalms were divided into five books, each concluding with Amen, or Hallelujah; the first ending with **Psalm 41**, the second with **Psalm 72**, the third with **Psalm 89**, the fourth with **Psalm 106**, the fifth with **Psalm 150**. Others divide them into three fifties; others into sixty parts, two for every day of the month, one for the morning, the other for the evening. Let good Christians divide them for themselves, so as may best increase their acquaintance with them, that they may have them at hand upon all occasions and may sing them in the spirit and with the understanding.

An Exposition of the Old and New Testament with Practical Remarks and Observations
Matthew Henry (1706)

The Book of Psalms

Psalm 1

This is a psalm of instruction concerning good and evil, setting before us life and death, the blessing and the curse, that we may take the right way which leads to happiness and avoid that which will certainly end in our misery and ruin. The different character and condition of godly people and wicked people, those that serve God and those that serve him not, is here plainly stated in a few words; so that every man, if he will be faithful to himself, may here see his own face and then read his own doom. That division of the children of men into saints and sinners, righteous and unrighteous, the children of God and the children of the wicked one, as it is ancient, ever since the struggle began between sin and grace, the seed of the woman and the seed of the serpent, so it is lasting, and will survive all other divisions and subdivisions of men into high and low, rich and poor, bond and free; for by this men's everlasting state will be determined, and the distinction will last as long as heaven and hell. This psalm shows us,

I. The holiness and happiness of a godly man (verses 1-3).

II. The sinfulness and misery of a wicked man (verse 4-5).

III. The ground and reason of both (verse 6).

Whoever collected the psalms of David (probably it was Ezra) with good reason put this psalm first, as a preface to the rest, because it is absolutely necessary to the acceptance of our devotions that we be righteous before

God (for it is only the prayer of the upright that is his delight), and therefore that we be right in our notions of blessedness and in our choice of the way that leads to it. Those are not fit to put up good prayers who do not walk in good ways.

Psalm 1:1-3

The psalmist begins with the character and condition of a godly man, that those may first take the comfort of that to whom it belongs. Here is,

I. A description of the godly man's spirit and way, by which we are to try ourselves. The Lord knows those that are his by name, but we must know them by their character; for that is agreeable to a state of probation, that we may study to answer to the character, which is indeed both the command of the law which we are bound in duty to obey and the condition of the promise which we are bound in interest to fulfill. The character of a good man is here given by the rules he chooses to walk by and to take his measures from. What we take at our setting out, and at every turn, for the guide of our conversation, whether the course of this world or the word of God, is of material consequence. An error in the choice of our standard and leader is original and fatal; but, if we be right here, we are in a fair way to do well.

1. A godly man, that he may avoid the evil, utterly renounces the companionship of evil-doers, and will not be led by them (verse 1); *He walks not in the council of the ungodly,* etc. This part of his character is put first, because those that will keep the commandments of their God must say to evil-doers, *Depart from us;* Psalm 119:115, and departing from evil is that in which wisdom begins.

(1). He sees evil-doers round about him; the world is full of them; they walk on every side. They are here described by three characters, *ungodly, sinners,* and *scornful.* See by what steps men arrive at the height of impiety. *Nemo repente fit turpissimus—None reach the height of vice at once.* They are ungodly first, casting off the fear of God and living in the neglect of their duty to him: but they rest not there. When the services of religion are laid aside, they come to be *sinners,* that is, they break out into open rebellion against God and engage in the service of sin and Satan. Omissions make way for commissions, and by these the

B
a
c
k

i
t

u
p

heart is so hardened that at length they come to be *scorners*, that is, they openly defy all that is sacred, scoff at religion, and make a jest of sin. Thus is the way of iniquity down-hill; the bad grow worse, sinners themselves become tempters to others and advocates for Baal. The word which we translate *ungodly* signifies such as are unsettled, aim at no certain end and walk by no certain rule, but are at the command of every lust and at the beck of every temptation. The word for *sinners* signifies such as are determined for the practice of sin and set it up as their trade. The *scornful* are those that set *their mouths against the heavens*. These the good man sees with a sad heart; they are a constant vexation to his righteous soul. But,

(2). He shuns them wherever he sees them. He does not do as they do; and, that he may not, he does not converse familiarly with them.

[1.] He does *not walk **in the counsel of the ungodly*** *[neglecting the fear and worship of God, or violating his commands]*. He is not present at their councils, nor does he advise with them; though they are ever so witty, and subtle, and learned, if they are ungodly, they shall not be the men of his counsel. He does *not consent* to them, nor *say as they say,* **Luke 23:51.** He does not take his measures from their principles, nor act according to the advice which they give and take. The ungodly are forward to give their advice against religion, and it is managed so artfully that we have reason to think ourselves happy if we escape being tainted and ensnared by it.

[2.] He **stands** not **in the way of sinners** *[one who has voluntarily disobeyed any divine precept, or neglected any known duty]*; he avoids doing as they do; their way shall not be his way; he will not come into it, much less will he continue in it, as the sinner does, who *sets himself in a way that is not good,* **Psalm 36:4.** He avoids (as much as may be) being where they are. That he may not imitate them, he will not associate with them, nor choose them for his companions. He does not stand in their way, to be picked up by them **Proverbs 7:8,** but keeps as far from them as from a place or person infected with the plague, for fear of the contagion, **Proverbs 4:14-15.** He that would be kept from harm must keep out of harm's way.

[3.] He **sits not in the seat of the scornful** [holding religion in contempt/ despising; treating with disdain religion and the dispensations/distributions of God]; he does not repose [lay at rest] himself with those that sit down secure in their wickedness and please themselves with the searedness of their own consciences. He does not associate with those that sit in close cabal [persons untied in some close design, usually to promote their private views] to find out ways and means for the support and advancement of the devil's kingdom, or that sit in open judgment, magisterially [arrogantly] to condemn the generation of the righteous. The seat of the drunkards is the *seat of the scornful*, **Psalm 69:12**. Happy is the man that never sits in it, **Hosea 7:5**.

2. A godly man, that he may do that which is good and cleave to it, submits to the guidance of the word of God and makes that familiar to him, verse 2. This is that which keeps him out of the way of the ungodly and fortifies him against their temptations. *By the words of your lips I have kept me from the path of the deceiver,* **Psalm 17:4**. We need not court [to flatter; to endeavor to please by civilities and address;] the fellowship of sinners, either for pleasure or for improvement, while we have fellowship with the word of God and with God himself in and by his word. *When you awake it shall talk with you,* **Proverbs 6:22**. We may judge of our spiritual state by asking, "What is the law of God to us? What account do we make of it? What place has it in us?' See here,

(1). The entire affection which a good man has for the law of God: **His delight is in** it. He delights in it, though it be a law, a yoke, because it is the law of God, which is holy, just, and good, which he freely consents to, and so delights in, *after the inner man,* **Romans 7:16, 22**. All who are well pleased that there is a God must be well pleased that there is a Bible, a revelation of God, of his will, and of the only way to happiness in him.

(2). The intimate acquaintance which a good man keeps up with the word of God: **In that law does he meditate day and night;** and by this it appears that his delight is in it, for what we love we love to think of, **Psalm 119:97**. To meditate in God's word is to discourse [communication of thoughts] with ourselves concerning the great things contained in it, with a close application of mind, a fixedness of thought, till we be suitably affected with those things and experience the savor *[character, quality, value, nature]* and power of them in our hearts. This we must do *day and night;* we must have a constant habitual regard to the word of God as the rule of our actions and the spring of our comforts, and we must have it in our thoughts, accordingly, upon every occasion that occurs, whether night or day. No time is amiss *[wrong; faulty; out of order; improper]* for meditating on the word of God, nor is any time unseasonable for those visits. We must not only set ourselves to meditate on God's word morning and evening, at the entrance of the day and of the night, but these thoughts should be interwoven with the business and converse of every day and with the repose and slumbers of every night. *When I awake I am still with you.* **Psalm 139:18**

II. An assurance given of the godly man's happiness, with which we should encourage ourselves to answer the character of such.

1. In general, he is **blessed** *[spiritual happiness and the favor of God]*, (v. 1) God blesses him, and that blessing will make him happy. Blessednesses are to him, blessings of all kinds, of the upper and nether springs, enough to make him completely happy; none of the ingredients of happiness shall be wanting to him. When the psalmist undertakes to describe a blessed man, he describes a good man; for, after all, those only are happy, truly happy, that are holy *[pure in heart, temper or dispositions; free from sin and sinful affections]*, truly holy; and we are more concerned to know the way to blessedness than to know wherein that blessedness will consist. Nay, goodness and holiness are not only the way to happiness **Revelation 22:14** but happiness itself; supposing there were not another life after this, yet that man is a happy man that keeps in the way of his duty.

2. His blessedness is here illustrated by a similitude *[likeness; resemblance]* (v. 3): *He shall be like a tree*, fruitful and flourishing. This is the effect,

(1). Of his pious *[due respect, honor and affection for the character and service of God]* practice; he meditates in the law of God, turns that in *succum et sanguinem—into juice and blood*, and that makes him like a tree. The more we converse with the word of God the better furnished we are for every good word and work. Or,

(2). Of the promised blessing; he is blessed of the Lord, and therefore *he shall be like a tree.* The divine *[pertaining to the true God]* blessing produces real effects. It is the happiness of a godly man,

[1.] That he is *planted* by the grace of God. These trees were by nature wild olives, and will continue so till they are grafted anew, and so planted by a power from above. Never any good tree grew of itself; *it is the planting of the Lord*, and therefore he must in it be glorified. Isaiah 61:3, *The trees of the Lord are full of sap.*

[2.] That he is placed by the means of grace, here called *the rivers of water*, those rivers which *make glad the city of our God*; Psalm 46:4; from these a good man receives supplies of strength and vigor, but in secret undiscerned *[not seen or discovered]* ways.

[3.] That his practices shall be fruit, abounding to a good account, Philippians 4:17. To those whom God first blessed he said, *Be fruitful*; Genesis 1:22, and still the comfort and honor of fruitfulness are a recompense for the labor of it. It is expected from those who enjoy the mercies of grace that, both in the temper of their minds and in the tenor of their lives, they comply with the intentions of that grace, and then they bring forth fruit. And, be it observed to the praise of the great dresser of the vineyard, they *bring forth their fruit* (that which is required of them) in due season, when it is most beautiful and most useful, improving every opportunity of doing good and doing it in its proper time.

[4.] That his profession shall be preserved from blemish and decay: *His leaf also shall not wither.* As to those who bring forth only the leaves of profession, without any good fruit, even their *leaf* will wither and they shall be as much ashamed of their profession as ever they were proud of it; but, if the word of God rule in the heart, that will keep the profession green, both to our comfort and to our credit; the laurels *[praise, symbol of victory]* thus won shall never wither.

[5.] That prosperity shall attend him wherever he goes, soul-prosperity. *Whatever he does*, in conformity to the law, it *shall prosper* and succeed to his mind, or above his hope.

In singing these verses, being duly affected with the malignant *[malicious,* heinous, virulent/poison] and dangerous nature of sin, the transcendent [excellent, superior] excellencies of the divine law, and the power and efficacy [production to effect] of God's grace, from which our fruit is found, we must teach and admonish [teach, warn] ourselves, and one another, to watch against sin and all approaches towards it, to converse much with the word of God, and abound in the fruit of righteousness; and, in praying over them, we must seek to God for his grace both to fortify us against every evil word and work and to furnish us for every good word and work.

Psalm 1:4-6

Here is,

I. The description of the ungodly given, (verse 4).

1. In general, they are the reverse of the righteous, both in character and condition: They are not so. The Septuagint [Greek version of the Old Testament] emphatically repeats this: *Not so* the ungodly; they are *not so*; they are led by the counsel of the wicked, [evil in principle or practice; deviating from the divine law; addicted to vice; sinful; immoral] in the way of sinners, to the seat of the scornful; they have no delight in the law of God, nor ever think of it; they bring forth no fruit but grapes of Sodom **Genesis 13, 18-19**; they cumber [arrest, concern, trouble, grieve] the ground.

2. In particular, whereas the righteous [one who is holy in heart, and observant of the divine commands in practice] are like valuable, useful, fruitful trees, *they* **are like the chaff** [the husks when separated from the corn, refuse, worthless matter] **which the wind drives away,** the very lightest of the chaff, the dust which the owner of the floor desires to have driven away, as not capable of being put to any use. Would you value them? Would you weigh them? They are like chaff, of no worth at all in God's account, how highly soever they may value themselves. Would you know the temper [disposition] of their minds? They are light and vain [having no substance, value or importance]; they have no substance in them, no solidity [moral firmness; soundness; strength; validity; truth]; they are easily driven to and fro by every wind and temptation, and have no steadfastness [firmness of mind or purpose]. Would you know their end? The wrath [holy and just indignation] of God will drive them away in their wickedness, as the wind does the chaff, which is never gathered nor looked after more. The chaff may be, for a while,

among the wheat; but he is coming whose *fan is in his hand* and who will *thoroughly purge* [cleanse or purify by separating] *his floor.* Those that by their own sin and folly make themselves as chaff will be found so before the whirlwind and fire of divine wrath **Psalm 35:5**, so unable to stand before it or to escape it, **Isaiah 17:13.**

II. The doom of the ungodly read, (verse 5).

1. They will be cast, upon their trial, as traitors [one who betrays his trust] convicted: *They shall **not stand in the judgment,*** that is, they shall be found guilty, shall hang down the head with shame and confusion, and all their pleas and excuses will be overruled as frivolous [of little weight, worth or importance]. There is a judgment to come, in which every man's present character and work, though ever so artfully concealed and disguised, shall be truly and perfectly discovered, and appear in their own colors, and accordingly every man's future state will be, by an irreversible sentence, determined for eternity. The ungodly must appear in that judgment, to receive according to the things done in the body. They may hope to come off, nay [not this alone], to come off with honor, but their hope will deceive them: They shall not stand in the judgment, so plain will the evidence be against them and so just and impartial [not favoring one party more than another; equitable] will the judgment be upon it.

2. They will be for ever shut out from the society of the blessed. *They shall not stand **in the congregation** [assembly] **of the righteous,*** that is, in the *judgment* (so some), that court wherein the saints [holy or godly person], as assessors with Christ, shall judge the world, those holy myriads [an immense number] with which he shall come to execute *judgment upon all,* **Jude 1:14; 1 Corinthians 6:2.** Or in *heaven. There* will be seen, shortly, *a general assembly of the church of the first-born, a congregation of the righteous,* of all the saints, and none but saints, and saints made perfect [complete], such a congregation of them as never was in this world, **2 Thessalonians 2:1.** The wicked shall not have a place in that congregation. Into the new Jerusalem none unclean nor unsanctified [not made holy/perfect] shall enter; they shall see the righteous enter into the kingdom, and themselves, to their everlasting vexation [plague, torment, affliction], thrust out, **Luke 13:27.** The wicked and profane [irreverent/lacking respect to any thing sacred, polluted], in this world, ridiculed the righteous and their congregation, despised them, and cared not for their company; justly therefore will they be for ever separated from them. Hypocrites *[one who assumes a false appearance]* in this world, under the disguise of a plausible *[superficially pleasing]* profession, may thrust themselves into the congregation of the righteous and remain undisturbed and undiscovered there; but Christ cannot be imposed upon, though his ministers may; the day is coming when he will *separate between the sheep and the goats, the tares [weeds] and the wheat;* see **Matthew 13:41, 49.** That *great day* (so the Chaldee *[Chaldean]* here calls it) will be a day of discovery, a day of distinction, and a day of final division. Then you shall return and discern between the righteous and the wicked, which here it is sometimes hard to do, **Malachi 3:18.**

III. The reason rendered of this different state of the godly and wicked, (verse 6).

1. God must have all the glory of the prosperity and happiness of the righteous. They are blessed because **the Lord knows** their **way;** he chose them into it, inclined them to choose it, leads and guides them in it, and orders all their steps.

2. Sinners must bear all the blame of their own destruction. *Therefore* the ungodly perish, because the very way in which they have chosen and resolved to walk leads directly to destruction; it naturally tends towards ruin and therefore must necessarily end in it. Or we may take it thus, **The Lord** approves and is well pleased with **the way of the righteous,** and therefore, under the influence of his gracious smiles, it shall prosper and end well; but he is angry at the way of the wicked, all they do is offensive to him, and therefore it **shall perish,** and they in it. It is certain that every man's judgment proceeds from the Lord, and it is well or ill *[bad, evil]* with us, and is likely to be so to all eternity, accordingly as we are or are not accepted of God. Let this support the drooping spirits of the righteous, that the Lord knows their way, knows their hearts **Jeremiah 12:3,** knows their secret devotions **Matthew 6:6,** knows their character, how much soever it is blackened and blemished by the reproaches of men, and will shortly make them and their way manifest before the world, to their immortal *[never ending]* joy and honor. Let this cast a damp *[depress, deaden, deject, weaken]* upon the security and jollity *[lively celebration]* of sinners, that their way, though pleasant now, will perish at last.

In singing these verses, and praying over them, let us possess ourselves with a holy dread *[great fear or apprehension of evil or danger]* of the wicked man's portion, and deprecate *[express deep sorrow]* it with a firm and lively expectation of the judgment to come, and stir up ourselves to prepare for it, and with a holy care to approve ourselves to God in every thing, entreating *[make an earnest request]* his favor with our whole hearts.

M. Henry's Commentary—noun *[comments, expositions, explanations, or illustrations of difficult and obscure passages; a book of comments or annotations.]*

_____

_____

_____

_____

_____

_____

_____

_____

_____

_____

_____

_____

_____

_____

_____

_____

_____

_____

_____

_____

_____

_____

Back it up

Memory Verse

Back it up

RenewingLives.com

Cross References noun *[reference to another scripture to confirm and compare truth.]* **Use scripture: 1) to interpret scripture, 2) as commentary upon itself.**

Psalm 1:1

Blessed
- ❏ Deuteronomy 28:2-68 ❏ Deuteronomy 33:29 ❏ Jeremiah 17:7
- ❏ Psalm 2:12 ❏ Psalm 32:1-2 ❏ Psalm 34:8 ❏ Psalm 84:12
- ❏ Psalm 106:3 ❏ Psalm 112:1 ❏ Psalm 115:12-15 ❏ Psalm 119:1,2
- ❏ Psalm 144:15 ❏ Psalm 146:5 ❏ Matthew 10:3 ❏ Matthew 13:55
- ❏ Matthew 16:17 ❏ Mark 3:18 ❏ Mark 6:3 ❏ Luke 6:16 ❏ Luke 11:28
- ❏ John 13:17 ❏ John 14:22 ❏ John 20:29 ❏ Acts 1:1 ❏ Revelation 22:14

walks
- ❏ Genesis 5:24 ❏ Leviticus 26:27-28 ❏ 1 Kings 16:31
- ❏ Job 31:5 ❏ Psalms 81:12 ❏ Proverbs 1:15 ❏ Proverbs 4:14-15
- ❏ Proverbs 13:20 ❏ Ezekiel 20:18 ❏ 1 Peter 4:3

counsel
- ❏ Genesis 49:6 ❏ 2 Chronicles 22:3 ❏ Job 10:3 ❏ Job 21:16 ❏ Psalm 64:2
- ❏ Luke 23:51

ungodly (wicked)
- ❏ Genesis 18:23, 25 ❏ Exodus 9:27 ❏ Exodus 23:1 ❏ Exodus 23:7
- ❏ Numbers 16:26 ❏ Deuteronomy 25:1-2 ❏ 1 Samuel 2:9
- ❏ 1 Samuel 24:13 ❏ 2 Samuel 4:11 ❏ 1 Kings 8:32 ❏ 2 Chronicles 6:23
- ❏ 2 Chronicles 19:2 ❏ Job 3:17 ❏ Psalm 3:7 ❏ Psalm 7:9 ❏ Psalm 9:5
- ❏ Psalm 9:16-17 ❏ Psalm 10:2-4 ❏ Psalm 10:13, 15 ❏ Psalm 11:2, 5-6
- ❏ Psalm 12:8 ❏ Psalm 17:9, 13 ❏ Psalm 26:5 ❏ Psalm 28:3 ❏ Psalm 31:17 ❏ Psalm 32:10 ❏ Psalm 34:21 ❏ Psalm 36:1 ❏ Psalm 36:11
- ❏ Psalm 37 ❏ Psalm 39:1 ❏ Psalm 50:16 ❏ Psalm 55:3 ❏ Psalm 58:3, 10
- ❏ Psalm 68:2 ❏ Psalm 71:4 ❏ Psalm 73:3, 12 ❏ Psalm 75:4, 8, 10
- ❏ Psalm 82:2, 4 ❏ Psalm 91:8 ❏ Psalm 92:7 ❏ Psalm 94:3 ❏ Psalm 94:13 ❏ Psalm 97:10 ❏ Psalm 101:8 ❏ Psalm 104:35 ❏ Psalm 106:18
- ❏ Psalm 109:2, 6-7 ❏ Psalm 112:10 ❏ Psalm 119:53, 61 ❏ Psalm 119:95, 110, 119, 155 ❏ Psalm 129:4 ❏ Psalm 139:19 ❏ Psalm 140:4, 8 ❏ Psalm 141:10 ❏ Psalm 145:20 ❏ Psalm 146:9 ❏ Psalm 147:6 ❏ Proverbs 2:22
- ❏ Proverbs 3:25, 33 ❏ Proverbs 4:14, 19 ❏ Proverbs 5:22 ❏ Proverbs 9:7 ❏ Proverbs 10 ❏ Proverbs 11 ❏ Proverbs 12 ❏ Proverbs 13
- ❏ Proverbs 14

Back it up

Cross References *(continued)*

- ❏ Proverbs 15 ❏ Proverbs 16:4 ❏ Proverbs 17:15, 23
- ❏ Proverbs 18:3, 5 ❏ Proverbs 19:28 ❏ Proverbs 20:26
- ❏ Proverbs 21:4, 7 ❏ Proverbs 21 ❏ Proverbs 24:15 ❏ Proverbs 24
- ❏ Proverbs 25:5, 26 ❏ Proverbs 28 ❏ Proverbs 29 ❏ Ecclesiastes 3:17
- ❏ Ecclesiastes 7:15 ❏ Ecclesiastes 8:10, 13-14 ❏ Ecclesiastes 9:2
- ❏ Isaiah 3:11 ❏ Isaiah 5:23 ❏ Isaiah 11:4 ❏ Isaiah 13:11 ❏ Isaiah 14:5
- ❏ Isaiah 26:10 ❏ Isaiah 48:22 ❏ Isaiah 53:9 ❏ Isaiah 55:7, 20-21
- ❏ Isaiah 57:20-21 ❏ Jeremiah 5:26 ❏ Jeremiah 12:1 ❏ Jeremiah 23:19
- ❏ Jeremiah 25:31 ❏ Jeremiah 30:23 ❏ Ezekiel 3:18-19 ❏ Ezekiel 7:21
- ❏ Ezekiel 13:22 ❏ Ezekiel 18 ❏ Ezekiel 21 ❏ Ezekiel 33 ❏ Daniel 12:10
- ❏ Micah 6:10 ❏ Habakkuk 1:4, 13 ❏ Habakkuk 3:13 ❏ Zephaniah 1:3
- ❏ Malachi 3:18 ❏ Malachi 4:3

stands
- ❏ Psalm 26:12 ❏ Romans 5:2 ❏ Ephesians 6:13

way
- ❏ Psalm 1:6 ❏ Psalm 36:4 ❏ Psalm 146:9 ❏ Proverbs 2:12
- ❏ Proverbs 4:19 ❏ Proverbs 13:15 ❏ Matthew 7:13-14

sits
- ❏ Psalm 26:4,5 ❏ Psalm 119:115 ❏ Jeremiah 15:17

scornful
- ❏ Proverbs 1:22 ❏ Proverbs 3:34 ❏ Proverbs 9:12 ❏ Proverbs 19:29

Psalm 1:2

But his
- ❏ Psalm 40:8 ❏ Psalm 112:1 ❏ Psalm 119:11 ❏ Psalm 119:35
- ❏ Psalm 119:47-48 ❏ Psalm 119:72 ❏ Psalm 119:92 ❏ Job 23:12
- ❏ Jeremiah 15:16 ❏ Romans 7:22 ❏ 1 John 5:3

meditate
- ❏ Psalm 104:34 ❏ Psalm 119:11 ❏ Psalm 119:15 ❏ Psalm 119:97-99
- ❏ Joshua 1:8 ❏ 1 Timothy 4:15

day
- ❏ Psalm 88:1 ❏ Luke 2:37 ❏ Luke 18:7 ❏ 1 Thessalonians 2:9
- ❏ 2 Timothy 1:3

Psalm 1:3

tree
- ❏ Job 14:9 ❏ Isaiah 44:4 ❏ Jeremiah 17:8 ❏ Ezekiel 17:8 ❏ Ezekiel 19:10

Back it up

Renewingminds.com

Cross References *(continued)*

❑ Ezekiel 47:12 ❑ Revelation 22:2

brings

❑ Psalm 92:14 ❑ Matthew 21:34 ❑ Matthew 21:41

shall not

❑ Isaiah 27:11 ❑ Matthew 13:6 ❑ Matthew 21:19 ❑ John 15:6 ❑ Jude 1:12

wither (fade)

❑ Psalm 1:3 ❑ Psalm 37:2 ❑ Isaiah 1:30 ❑ Isaiah 19:6-7 ❑ Isaiah 24:4
❑ Isaiah 28:1 ❑ Isaiah 28:4 ❑ Isaiah 34:4 ❑ Isaiah 40:7-8 ❑ Isaiah 64:6
❑ Jeremiah 8:13 ❑ Jeremiah 14:21 ❑ Ezekiel 47:12

whatsoever

❑ Genesis 39:3 ❑ Genesis 39:23 ❑ Joshua 1:7-8 ❑ 1 Chronicles 22:11
❑ 2 Chronicles 31:21 ❑ 2 Chronicles 32:23 ❑ Psalm 128:2 ❑ Psalm 129:8
❑ Isaiah 3:10

Psalm 1:4

like

❑ Psalm 35:5 ❑ Job 21:18 ❑ Isaiah 17:13 ❑ Isaiah 29:5 ❑ Hosea 13:3
❑ Matthew 3:12

Psalm 1:5

shall

❑ Psalm 5:5 ❑ Psalm 24:3 ❑ Luke 21:36 ❑ Jude 1:15

sinners

❑ Psalm 26:9 ❑ Malachi 3:18 ❑ Matthew 13:49 ❑ Matthew 25:32
❑ Matthew 25:41 ❑ Matthew 25:46

Psalm 1:6

knows

❑ Psalm 37:18-24 ❑ Psalm 139:1-2 ❑ Psalm 142:3 ❑ Job 23:10
❑ Nahum 1:7 ❑ John 10:14 ❑ John 10:27 ❑ 2 Timothy 2:19

way

❑ Psalm 26:9 ❑ Psalm 112:10 ❑ Psalm 146:9 ❑ Proverbs 14:12
❑ Proverbs 15:9 ❑ Malachi 3:18 ❑ Matthew 13:49 ❑ Matthew 25:32
❑ Matthew 25:41 ❑ Matthew 25:46

ungodly/wicked

See Psalm 1:1 references

perish

❑ Psalm 9:6 ❑ Psalm 112:10 ❑ Proverbs 14:12

Back it up

Define each line—Instructions

Pay attention to the Strong's number that follows each word or phrase to the right, *e.g.,* H2454. Using the Dictionary/Lexicon/Strong's resource, which begins on page 96, record the definition of each word on the lines provided.

When you read God's word with a better understanding of what the words mean in context, you'll be closer to a reasonable interpretation of the text.

Breaking down the verse, word/phrase-by-word/phrase takes time but is useful to ponder the meanings and commit them to memory.

If you have the opportunity to share or teach God's word, your finished work will come in handy.

EXAMPLE

14 **:1 Every wise** H2454 f-noun Discerning, judging correctly, discriminating between true/false: proper/improper

woman H802 f-noun female: wife: woman

the female of the human race grown to adult years

builds H1129 verb erects a house, walls, defenses, restores: rebuilds: gives/begets offspring

her house: H1004 proper patrial adjective, adverb, m-noun family: inside: place: within: palace, fortress; dwelling: abode: habitation

but the foolish H200 f-noun silly: ungodliness: one void of understanding or sound judgment: weak in intellect: marked with folly

plucks it down H2040 verb pulls down or in pieces: breaks: destroys: overthrows: ruins

with her hands. H3027 f-noun the open one (hand) indicating power, means, direction, etc., the hand being the seat of strength

2 He that walks H1980 verb to go along, with, through: to live, follow any manner of life: to go forward

in his uprightness H3476 m-noun straightness of way: what is right: what ought to be done: that which is just, meet, true

fears H3373 adjective reverences (fear mingled with affection, respect and esteem): a holy awe or reverence of God and his laws

the LORD: H3068 proper noun with reference to deity (the) self-Existent or Eternal: Jeho-vah/Yeho-vah: the Supreme God: the Supreme Being

but he that is perverse H3868 verb to turn aside, distorted from the right, obstinate in the wrong, froward, to go back, perverted: wicked

in his ways H1870 m-noun a road trodden: ac ourse of life or mode of action: custom: manner: the action of going, journey one takes

B a c k i t u p

Intro to Biblical Hebrew Verbs

The process of indentifying a Biblical Hebrew verb's root, stem, and conjugation is called "**Parsing.**" Biblical Hebrew is primarily a verbal language. The following is a *very brief and incomplete* introduction. Hopefully, it will inspire you to study further.

Biblical Hebrew verbs have a:

(1) **Root** Shoresh

(2) Binyanim: **Stem**

Pa'al Qal *simple action/active voice*
Niphal *simple/passive or reflective*
Piel *intensive/active*
Pual *intensive/passive*
Hiphil *causative/active*
Hophal *causative/passive*
Hithpael *intensive/reflexive*

(3) **Conjugation** (inflection)

Cohortative *[expresses a command, purpose, request, result, or wish (in the 1st person).]*
Imperative *[expresses a direct command that demands immediate action from the one being addressed (in the 2nd person).]*
Imperfect *[generally, a future, incomplete or ongoing action.]*
Infinitive Absolute *[used in conjunction with other verbs, it emphasizes or intensifies the verbal action. It is sometimes put in place of an Imperative to express a command. It has no English counterpart.]*

Infinitive Construct *[functions like an English Infinitive with use of the preposition "to" plus the verb, e.g., to write.]*
Jussive *[used to express a mild command or strong wish (in the 3rd person).]*
Participle *[a verbal adjective constructed from a verb which functions like an adjective.]*
Perfect *[generally a completed action.]*

and most have a:

(A) **Aspect:** causal, intensive, simple

(B) **Gender:** feminine, masculine, feminine or masculine

(C) **Person:** I (1st person), you (2nd person), we (3rd person)

(D) **Number:** singular (one) or plural (more than one)

(E) **Tense** (determined by context)

(F) **Voice** (active, middle, passive).

For example, in Psalm 1:1—
Blessed is the man that walks *qal perfect*
Qal *simple (not reflexive—something in the past or causal—expressing a cause or reason)*
active (the subject does the action)
Perfect *[a completed action]*

Walks is the verb. It is an active action (the doer, not the receiver of). In Psalm 1:1, the man that wants to be happy walks opposite of "the counsel of the ungodly," "standing in the way of sinners," or "sitting in the seat of the scornful."

Define each line

1:1 Blessed H835 m-noun

is the man H376 m-noun

that walks H1980 verb: *qal perfect*

not in the counsel H6098 f-noun

of the ungodly, H7563 adjective

nor stands H5975 verb: *qal perfect*

in the way H1870 m-noun

of sinners, H2400 adjective, m-noun

nor sits H3427 verb: *qal perfect*

in the seat H4186 m-noun

of the scornful. H3887 verb *qal participle*

2 But his delight H2656 m-noun

is in the law H8451 f-noun

of the LORD; H3068 proper noun ref. to deity

and in his law H8451 f-noun

does he meditate H1897 verb: *qal imperfect*

day H3119 adverb, substantive

and night. H3915 m-noun

3 And he shall be like a tree H6086 m-noun

planted H8362 verb *qal passive participle*

by the rivers H6388 m-noun

of water, H4325 m-noun

that brings forth H5414 verb: *qal imperfect*

his fruit H6529 m-noun

in his season; H6256 f-noun

his leaf H5929 m-noun

Define each line

also shall not wither; H5034 verb: *qal imperfect*

and whatsoever he does H6213 verb: *qal imperfect*

shall prosper. H6743 verb: *qal imperfect*

4 The ungodly H7563 adjective

are not so: but are like the chaff H4671 m-noun

which the wind H7307 f-noun

drives away. H5086 verb: *qal imperfect*

5 Therefore the ungodly H7563 adjective

shall not stand H6965 verb: *qal imperfect*

in the judgment, H4941 m-noun

nor sinners H2400 adjective, m-noun

in the congregation H5712 f-noun

of the righteous. H6662 adjective

B
a
c
k

i
t

u
p

6 For the LORD H3068 proper noun ref. to deity

knows H3045 verb *qal passive participle*

the way H1870 m-noun

of the righteous: H6662 adjective

but the way H1870 m-noun

of the ungodly H7563 adjective

shall perish. H6 verb: *qal imperfect*

Dictionary, Lexicon & Strong's

This study provides basic definitions used in Psalm 1, including Hebrew root words. A definition is a brief statement of the meaning of a word, usually compiled in a dictionary. A lexicon helps explain the significance of a word or phrase and what it is understood to express. A Bible concordance provides an alphabetical index of words and a reference to the verse in which it occurs. The following pages compile all three into one source of information.

You'll find the dictionary, lexicons, and Strong's notes do not specify the exact *single* meaning of a word but list many words that *could* apply in the given passage. The definitions contained in this book do not tell you which word is appropriate amongst the many words and choices, nor does it tell you how the word is used. If you are just starting out in Bible study, you'll tend to pick the meaning you like or the one that makes sense to you.

A student of the Bible needs to study the context of the verse over the possible meanings that could be applied. The word "context" means *the parts of a discourse* [a communication of thoughts by words] *which precede or follow the sentence quoted; the passages* [portion of a written work—sentence, verse, one or more paragraphs] *of scripture which are near the text, either before it or after it.*

When interpreting the Bible, there are many things to consider, including alternate meanings, context, common words and phrases, cultural references, idioms, metaphors, references to historical events, speech, time periods, and word study, including parsing, spelling, and root word etymology.

The precise meaning of each word within a specific verse requires a serious commitment to biblical "word study" "in context," which is often done by Bible scholars and linguists practiced in etymology [explaining the origin and derivation of words] and hermeneutics [finding the meaning of an author's words and phrases, and of explaining it to others.].

As you continue in word study, you'll find there is so much more to understanding the words in the Bible and how they are to be interpreted and applied in each sentence.

Sources & Definition Key

An American Dictionary of the English Language (1828) Noah Webster Jr. Mr. Webster established a system of rules to govern spelling, grammar, and reading, using the Bible as the foundation for his definitions. He considered education without the Bible "useless."

Gesenius's Hebrew and Chaldee Lexicon Wilhelm Gesenius (1786–1842) Professor and Bible scholar. Gesenius was a German-born master of Hebrew. Upon his passing, his documents were edited and translated into English by Samuel P. Tregelles (1813-1875).

Strong's Exhaustive Concordance of the Bible (1890) with dictionaries. This concordance provides an index of every word in the King James Version (KJV) and assigns a "Strong's number" to the root words. It provides the transliteration, which means it converts a word from a different language into letters you can understand (such as from Hebrew to English). It also provides the etymology showing how a simple root word developed to the word used at the time of translation. It should not be considered sufficient for hermeneutics, which is the principle of interpreting and expounding the Scriptures, but it can be a starting point.

> **Strong's Legend:** The small × is used to signify a rendering that is a result of an idiom peculiar to the Greek or Hebrew. [] Brackets are used if there is an inclusion of an additional word in Greek or Hebrew.

Note: This workbook does not provide a full word study education. Avoid taking a hard stance on the exact meaning of words based on this book alone. It should get you close, *but not close enough without further research.*

---

i.e.=Is an abbreviation of the Latin phrase *id est*, meaning "**that is.**" It is used to clarify or reword.

e.g.=Is an abbreviation of the Latin phrase *exempli gratia*, meaning "for example." You can remember is as "**example given.**" It is used to illustrate what has been stated.

B a c k i t u p

Definition Key

→

H1
The original language **A**=Aramaic, **H**=Hebrew, **G**=Greek, followed by the Strong's number assigned.

Father
Word used in the Scriptures.

אָב
Hebrew spelling.

'āḇ
The transliteration of Hebrew to English.

awb
Close pronunciation.

1215X
Number of times it is found in the King James Version.

masculine noun
Part of Speech in English.

Definition within a definition
[shown like this].

S=
Strong's Concordance Dictionary

LB=
Lexicon: Brown-Driver-Briggs

LG=
Lexicon: Gesenius' Hebrew-Chaldee

W=
Webster's 1828 Dictionary

H1 *Father* אָב 'āḇ *awb* 1215X **masculine noun**
S= a primitive *[a word not derived from another]* word; father, in a literal and immediate, or figurative and remote application:—chief, (fore-) father(-less), × patrimony, principal. **LG=** 1. Used of any ancestor. 2. Used of the founder, or first ancestor. 3. Used of the author, or maker of anything, specially of the Creator, Job 38:28. 4. It is applied to a bringer, nourisher, bestowing his benefits like a parent, Job 29:16. 5. It is used of a master, or teacher, 1 Samuel 10:12. 6. Specially the father of the king, a name given to his supreme counsellor, Genesis 45:8. 7. It is further used to express intimate connection and relationship, Job 17:14. 8. In arabic is applied to a possessor, as one who is endued with anything or excels in it, in Hebrew "father of peace" meaning peaceful. **W=** 1. He who begets a child; in Latin, a genitor or generator, Proverbs 17:21. 2. The first ancestor; the progenitor of a race or family. 3. The appellation of an old man, and a term of respect, 2 Kings 6:21. 4. The grandfather or more remote ancestor, Daniel 5:2. 5. One who feeds and supports, or exercises paternal care over another, Psalms 118:1. 6. He who creates, invents, makes or composes any thing; the author, former or contriver; a founder, director or instructor, John 8:16. Satan is called the father of lies; he introduced sin, and instigates men to sin, John 8:16. Abraham is called the father of believers. He was an early believer, and a pattern of faith and obedience, Romans 4:1. 7. Fathers, in the plural, ancestors, 1 Kings 2:12. 8. A father in law, Luke 3:8. 9. The appellation of the first person in the adorable Trinity, Matthew 28:19.

Back it up

Dictionary, Lexicon & Strong's

H6 *perish* אָבַד '*āḇaḏ aw-bad'* 184x **verb S=** A primitive root; properly, to wander away, i.e. lose oneself; by implication to perish (causative, destroy):— break, destroy, destruction, not escape, fail, lose, (cause to, make) perish, spend, × and surely, take, be undone, × utterly, be void of, have no way to flee. **LG=** 1. To be lost, to lose oneself, to wander. 2. Figurative, cause to vanish, blot out, do away with. 3. Cause to stray, lose. **W=** PER'ISH, **verb intransitive** [literally, to depart wholly.] 1. To die; to lose life in any manner; applied to animals. 2. To die; to wither and decay; applied to plants. 3. To waste away; as, a leg or an arm has perished. 4. To be in a state of decay or passing away. 5. To be destroyed; to come to nothing. 6. To fail entirely or to be extirpated. 2 Kings 9:8. 7. To be burst or ruined. Luke 5:37. 8. To be wasted or rendered useless. Jeremiah 9:12. 9. To be injured or tormented. 1 Corinthians 8:11. 10. To be lost eternally; to be sentenced to endless misery. 2 Peter 2:12.

H376 *man* אִישׁ '*îš eesh'* 1639x **masculine-noun S=** Contracted for H582 (or perhaps rather from an unused root meaning to be extant); a man as an individual or a male person; often used as an adjunct to a more definite term (and in such cases frequently not expressed in translation):—also, another, any (man), a certain, champion, consent, each, every (one), fellow, (foot-, husband-) man, (good-, great, mighty) man, he, high (degree), him (that is), husband, man(-kind), none, one, people, person, steward, what (man) soever, whoso(-ever), worthy. **LG=** 1. A man, specially as opposed to a woman, a male. 2. One, another. 3. Anyone, someone. 4. Each, every one. 5. One or men. 6. Sons of men. **W=** MAN, **noun** [species, kind, image, similitude.] 1. Mankind; the human race; the whole species of human beings; beings distinguished from all other animals by the powers of reason and speech, as well as by their shape and dignified aspect. Genesis 1:26, Job 14:1. In the System of Nature, man is ranked as a distinct genus. 2. A male individual of the human race, of

Back it up

Renewing Lives.com

adult growth or years. 3. A male of the human race. 4. A servant, or an attendant of the male sex. 5. A word of familiar address. 6. It sometimes bears the sense of a male adult of some uncommon qualifications; particularly, the sense of strength, vigor, bravery, virile powers, or magnanimity, as distinguished from the weakness, timidity or impotence of a boy, or from the narrow mindedness of low bred men. 1 Samuel 17:8 7. An individual of the human species. 8. Man is sometimes opposed to boy or child, and sometimes to beast. 9. One who is master of his mental powers, or who conducts himself with his usual judgment. 10. It is sometimes used indefinitely, without reference to a particular individual; any person; one. 11. In popular usage, a husband.

H518 *in* אִם ʻim *eem* 43x **particle S=** A **primitive particle**; used very widely as **demonstrative**, lo!; **interrogative**, whether?; or **conditional**, if, although; also Oh that!, when; hence, as a negative, not:—(and, can-, doubtless, if, that) (not), + but, either, + except, + more(-over if, than), neither, nevertheless, nor, oh that, or, + save (only, -ing), seeing, since, sith, + surely (no more, none, not), though, + of a truth, + unless, + verily, when, whereas, whether, while, + yet. **LG=** A **demonstrative**, **interrogative**, and **conditional particle**. 1. **Demonstrative** as in: lo! behold! In direct **interrogation**: whether... or, if... whether. 2. **Particle** of conceding: though, although. 3. **Particle** of wishing: oh that! would that! 4. **Particle** of time: when. 5. It is rarely: that, since. **W=** IN, **prefix**, Latin IN is used in composition as a particle of negation, like the English un, of which it seems to be a dialectical orthography; or it denotes within, into, or among, such as inbred, incase; or it serves only to augment or render emphatical the sense of the word to which it is prefixed, such as inclose, increase. IN, before l, is changed into il, as in illusion; and before r, into ir, as in irregular; and into im, before a labial, such as imbitter, immaterial, impatient. IN, **preposition** denotes present or inclosed, surrounded by limits; as in a house. It denotes a state of being mixed, as sugar in tea. It denotes present in any state; as in sickness or health. It denotes present in time; as in that hour or day. IN the name, is used in

Back it up

phrases of invoking, swearing, declaring, praying, etc. in prayer. IN, in many cases, is equivalent to on. This use of the word is frequent in the Scriptures; as, let fowls multiply in the earth. IN signifies by or through: in thee shall all nations be blessed. IN that, is sometimes equivalent to because: Some things they do in that they are men; some things in that they are men misled and blinded with error. IN these and similar phrases, that is an antecedent, substitute, or pronoun relating to the subsequent part of the sentence, or the subsequent clause. God commendeth his love towards us, in that while we were yet sinners, Christ died for us. That is, in the fact stated in the latter clause, for which that is the substitute. Romans 5:2. IN as much, seeing; seeing that; this being the fact. IN is often used without the noun to which it properly belongs. I care not who is in or who is out, that is, in office, or out of office.

H834 *that* אֲשֶׁר 'ăšer ash-er'
111X **conjunction, relative pronoun**
S= A **primitive relative pronoun** (of every gender and number); who, which, what, that; also (as an **adverb** and a **conjunction**) when, where, how, because, in order that, etc.:—× after, × alike, as (soon as), because, × every, for, + forasmuch, + from whence, + how(-soever), × if, (so) that (thing) which, wherein), × though, + until, + whatsoever, when, where (+ -as, -in, -of, -on, -soever, -with), which, whilst, + whither(-soever), who(-m, -soever, -se). As it is indeclinable, it is often accompanied by the **personal pronoun** expletively, used to show the connection.
LG= A. A **relative pronoun** of both genders and numbers: who, which, that. 1. Before the **relative**, the **pronoun**: he, she, it, is often omitted, e.g. Numbers 22:6 "and he whom thou curest;" B. It becomes a **conjunction**, 1. After **verbs** of seeing, hearing, etc. 2. Indicates design and purpose followed by a future, e.g. in order that. 3. Causal: because that, because followed by a **preterite**. e.g. Genesis 30:18. 4. **Conditional**, if, e.g.Leviticus 4:22. 5. At what time, when, followed by a **preterite**. e.g. Deuteronomy 11:6. 6. Where, whither, whithersoever. 7. As, like as, how, in what way, e.g. Job 37:17. As a sign of **apodosis**: then, so. **W=** THAT, an **adjective, pronoun** or **substitute**. 1. THAT is a word used as a **definitive adjective**, pointing to a certain person or thing

Back it up

before mentioned, or supposed to be understood. Matthew 10:14. 2. THAT is used definitively, to designate a specific thing or person emphatically. Matthew 9:6. In these cases, THAT is an **adjective**. 3. THAT is used as the representative of a **noun**, either a person or a thing. In this use, it is often a **pronoun** and a **relative**. Proverbs 9:4, Psalm 63:9. 4. THAT is also the representative of a sentence or part of a sentence, and often of a series of sentences. In this case, THAT is not strictly a **pronoun**, a word standing for a **noun**; but is, so to speak, a **pro-sentence**, the substitute for a sentence, to save the repetition of it. Leviticus 10:3, 1 Corinthians 6:2, Genesis 18:5. 5. THAT sometimes is the substitute for an **adjective**. 6. THAT in the following use, has been called a **conjunction**. 'I heard that the Greeks had defeated the Turks.' But in this case, that has the same character as in Number 4. It is the representative of the part of the sentence which follows, as may be seen by inverting the order of the clauses. 7. THAT was formerly used for that which, like what, John 3:2. [This use is no longer held legitimate.] 8. THAT is used in opposition to *this*, or by way of distinction. 9. When *this* and THAT refer to foregoing words, *this* refers to the latter, and THAT to the former. It is the same with *these* and *those*. 10. THAT sometimes introduces an explanation of something going before. 'Religion consists in living up to those principles; that is, in acting in conformity to them.' Here THAT refers to the whole first clause of the sentence. 11. When THAT begins a sentence, 'That we may fully understand the subject, let us consider the following propositions.' THAT denotes purpose, or rather introduces the clause expressing purposes.

H835 *blessed* אֶשֶׁר 'ešer *eh'-sher* 45X **masculine-noun S=** From H833; happiness; only in masculine plural construction as **interjection**, how happy!; blessed, happy. **LG=** O happy man! **W=** BLESS'ED **participle passive** Made happy or prosperous; extolled; pronounced happy. BLESS'ED **adjective** Happy; prosperous in worldly affairs; enjoying spiritual happiness and the favor of God; enjoying heavenly felicity.

H1870 *way* דֶּרֶךְ derek *deh'-rek* 705X **masculine-noun S=** From H1869; a road (as trodden);

Dictionary, Lexicon & Strong's

figuratively, a course of life or mode of action, often **adverb:**— along, away, because of, by, conversation, custom, eastward, journey, manner, passenger, through, toward, highway, pathway, wayside, whither, whithersoever. **LG=** 1. Properly, the action of going, walking, a going, hence a journey which anyone takes. 2. A way, path in which one goes. 3. Way, mode, course in which one goes or which one follows. **W=** WAY, **noun** 1. Literally, a passing; hence, a passage; the place of passing; hence, a road of any kind; a highway; a private road; a lane; a street; any place for the passing of men; cattle or other animals; a word of very comprehensive signification. 2. Length of space; as a great way; a little way. 3. Course; direction of motion or travel. 4. Passage; room for passing. 5. Course, or regular course. 6. Tendency to any meaning or act. 7. Sphere of observation. 8. Manner of doing any thing; method; means of doing. 9. Method; scheme of management. 10. Manner of thinking or behavior; particular turn of opinion; determination or humor. 11. Manner; mode. In no way does this matter belong to me. 12. Method; manner of practice. 13. Method or plan of life and conduct. Proverbs 3:17, Genesis 6:12. 14. Course; process of things, good or bad. 15. Right method to act or know. 16. General scheme of acting. 17. Ways, **plural,** in Scripture, the ways of God, are his providential government, or his works. Romans 11:33. Job 11:1.

H1897 *meditate* הָגָה hāḡâ *haw- gaw'* 25X **verb S=** A primitive root (compare H1901); to murmur (in pleasure or anger); by implication, to ponder:—imagine, meditate, mourn, mutter, roar, × sore, speak, study, talk, utter. **LG=** 1. To murmur, to mutter, to growl. 2. Poetically, to speak. 3 to meditate (property to speak with oneself, murmuring and in a low voice, as is often done by those who are musing. **W=** MED'ITATE, **verb intransitive** 1. To dwell on any thing in thought; to contemplate; to study; to turn or revolve any subject in the mind. Psalm 1:2. 2. To intend; to have in contemplation. MED'ITATE, **verb transitive** To plan by revolving in the mind; to contrive; to intend. 1. To think on; to revolve in the mind.

H1961 *be* הָיָה hāyâ *haw-yaw* 75X **verb S=** a primitive root

Back it up

(compare H1933); to exist, i.e. be or become, come to pass (always emphatic, and not a mere copula or auxiliary):— beacon, × altogether, be(-come), accomplished, committed, like), break, cause, come (to pass), do, faint, fall, follow, happen, × have, last, pertain, quit (one-) self, require, × use. **LG=** 1. To be, to exist, to become, to be made or done, to come to pass. **W=** BE, **verb intransitive substantive, participle present tense** being; **participle passive** been.[The sense is to stand, remain or be fixed; hence to continue. This **verb** is defective, and its defects are supplied by **verbs** from other roots, as, is, was, were, which have no radical connection with be.] 1. To be fixed; to exist; to have a real state or existence, for a longer or shorter time. Philippians 2:1. 2. To be made to be; to become. Mathhew 19, Jeremiah 32:4. 3. To remain. Let the garment be as it was made. 4. To be present in a place. 5. To have a particular manner of being or happening.

H1980 *walks* הָלַךְ hālak *haw- lak'* 25X **verb S=** Akin to H3212; a primitive root; to walk (in a great variety of applications, literally and figuratively):—(all) along, apace, behave (self), come, (on) continually, be conversant, depart, be eased, enter, exercise (self), follow, forth, forward, get, go (about, abroad, along, away, forward, on, out, up and down), greater, grow, lead, march, × more and more, move (self), needs, on, pass (away), be at the point, quite, run (along), send, speedily, spread, still, surely, tale-bearer, travel(-ler), walk (abroad, on, to and fro, up and down, to places), wander, wax, (way-) faring man, × be weak, whirl. **LG=** 1. To go, to walk, to go along. Used also of inanimate things, e.g. Genesis 7:18. The place towards which one is going. 2. To walk, i.e. to live, to follow any manner of life, e.g. Psalm 1:1 "walks (lives) according to the counsel of the wicked." 3. To go away, to vanish, e.g. Psalm 78:39. 4. To go, as water, e.g. to flow, to be poured out, e.g. Isaiah 8:7. 5. To go on, to go forward in any thing. **W=** WALK, verb intransitive [to full, to felt hats; a fuller; to stir, to be agitated, to rove, to travel, to wander, to roll. Our ancestors appropriated the verb to moving on the feet, and the word is peculiarly expressive of that rolling or wagging motion which marks

Back it up

the walk of clownish people.]
1. To move slowly on the feet; to step slowly along; to advance by steps moderately repeated; as animals. Daniel 4:37. 2. To move or go on the feet for exercise or amusement. 3. To appear, as a specter. 4. To act on any occasion. 5. To be in motion, as a clamorous tongue. 6. To act or move on the feet in sleep. 7. To range; to be stirring. 8. To move off; to depart. 9. In Scripture, to live and act or behave; to pursue a particular course of life. To walk with God, to live in obedience to his commands, and have communion with him. Genesis 5:22. To walk in darkness, to live in ignorance, error and sin, without comfort. 1 John 1:6. To walk in the light, to live in the practice of religion, and to enjoy its consolations. 1 John 1:7. To walk by faith, to live in the firm belief of the gospel and its promises, and to rely on Christ for salvation. 2 Corinthians 5:7. To walk through the fire, to be exercised with severe afflictions. Isaiah 43:2. To walk after the flesh, to indulge sensual appetites, and to live in sin. Romans 8:1. To walk after the Spirit, to be guided by the counsels and influences of the Spirit and by the word of God, and

to live a life of holy deportment. To walk in the flesh, to live this natural life, which is subject to infirmities and calamities. 2 Corinthians 10:3. WALK, **verb transitive** 1. To pass through or upon; as, to walk the streets. [This is elliptical for to walk in or through the street.] 2. To cause to walk or step slowly; to lead, drive or ride with a slow pace. WALK, **noun** 1. The act of walking; the act of moving on the feet with a slow pace. 2. The act of walking for air or exercise. 3. Manner of walking; gait; step. 4. Length of way or circuit through which one walks; or a place for walking. 5. An avenue set with trees. 6. Way; road; range; place of wandering. 7. Region; space. 8. Course of life or pursuit. 9. The slowest pace of a horse, ox, or other quadruped.

H2400 *sinners* חַטָּא ḥaṭṭā' *khat- taw'* 18x **adjective, masculine noun S=** Intensively from H2398; a criminal, or one accounted guilty:—offender, sinful, sinner. **LB=** 1. sinful. 2. sinners feminine adjective Amos 9:8 adjective a. sinful men Numbers 32:14, kingdom Amos 9:8. b. exposed to condemnation, reckoned as offenders 1 Kings 1:21. 2. noun masculine sinners. **LG=** 1. A sinner,

Back it up

Genesis 13:13. 2. One who bears blame, one counted culpable, 1 Kings 1:21. **W=** SIN'NER, noun 1. One that has voluntarily violated the divine law; a moral agent who has voluntarily disobeyed any divine precept, or neglected any known duty. 2. It is used in contradistinction to saint, to denote an unregenerate person; one who has not received the pardon of his sins. 3. an offender; a criminal. SIN'NER, verb intransitive To act as a sinner; in ludicrous language.

H2656 *delight* חֵפֶץ ḥēp̄eṣ

khay'- fets 39x **masculine noun S=** pleasure; hence (abstractly) desire; concretely, a valuable thing; hence (by extension) a matter (as something in mind):— acceptable, delight(-some), desire, things desired, matter, pleasant(-ure), purpose, willingly. **LG=** 1. Delight 2. Desire, will, Job 31:16. 3. Something precious, Isaiah 54:12. **W=** DELIGHT, **noun** 1. A high degree of pleasure, or satisfaction of mind; joy. Psalm 1:2. 2. That which gives great pleasure; that which affords delight. Proverbs 8:30. DELIGHT, **verb transitive** 1. To affect with great pleasure; to please highly; to give or afford high satisfaction or joy; as, a

beautiful landscape delights the eye; harmony delights the ear; the good conduct of children, and especially their piety, delights their parents. Psalm 1:2 2. To receive great pleasure in Psalm 40:8. DELIGHT, **verb intransitive** To have or take great pleasure; to be greatly pleased or rejoiced; followed by in. Romans 7:22.

H3045 *knows* יָדַע yāḏa *yaw-dah'*

947x **verb S=** A primitive root; to know (properly, to ascertain by seeing); used in a great variety of senses, figuratively, literally, euphemistically and inferentially (including observation, care, recognition; and causatively, instruction, designation, punishment, etc.):—acknowledge, acquaintance(-ted with), advise, answer, appoint, assuredly, be aware, (un-) awares, can(-not), certainly, comprehend, consider, × could they, cunning, declare, be diligent, (can, cause to) discern, discover, endued with, familiar friend, famous, feel, can have, be (ig-) norant, instruct, kinsfolk, kinsman, (cause to let, make) know, (come to give, have, take) knowledge, have (knowledge), (be, make, make to be, make self) known, be learned, lie by man, mark, perceive, privy to,

× prognosticator, regard, have respect, skilful, shew, can (man of) skill, be sure, of a surety, teach, (can) tell, understand, have (understanding), × will be, wist, wit, wot. **LG=** To perceive, to acquire knowledge, to know, to be acquainted. 1. To know, to perceive, to be aware of, often by the mind and hence to understand Judges 13:21. 2. To get to know, to discover, to know by experience, to experience, Job 5:25. **W=** KNOW, **verb transitive** knew; **participle passive** known. The radical sense of knowing is generally to take, receive, or hold.] 1. To perceive with certainty; to understand clearly; to have a clear and certain perception of truth, fact, or any thing that actually exists. To know a thing precludes all doubt or uncertainty of its existence. We know that truth and falsehood express ideas incompatible with each other. We know that a circle is not a square. 2. To be informed of; to be taught. 3. To distinguish; as, to know one man from another. 4. To recognize by recollection, remembrance, representation or description. 5. To be no stranger to; to be familiar. 6. In scripture, to have sexual commerce with. Genesis 4:1. 7. To

approve. Psalm 1:6. 8. To learn. Proverbs 1:2. 9. To acknowledge with due respect. 1 Thessalonians 5:2. 10. To choose; to favor or take an interest in. Amos 3:10. 11. To commit; to have. 2 Corinthians 12. To have full assurance of; to have satisfactory evidence of any thing, though short of certainty. KNOW, **verb intransitive** 1. To have clear and certain perception; not to be doubtful; sometimes with of. John 7:17. 2. To be informed. 3. To take cognizance of; to examine.

H3068 *LORD* יְהֹוָה Yᵉhōvâ *yeh-ho-vaw'* 6519x **proper noun with reference to deity S=** From H1961; (the) self-Existent or Eternal; Jeho-vah, Jewish national name of God:—Jehovah, the Lord. Compare H3050, H3069. **LG=** Proper name of the supreme God amongst the Hebrews. The later Hebrews, for some centuries before the time of Christ, either misled by a false interpretation of certain laws (Exodus 20:7; Leviticuas 24:11), or else following some old supersition, regarded this name as so very holy, that it might not even be prounounced. **W=** LORD, **noun** 1. A master; a person possessing supreme power and authority; a ruler; a governor. 2. A husband. Genesis 18:1. 4. In scripture, the

Supreme Being; Jehovah. When lord in the Old Testament, it prints in capitals, it is the translation of JEHOVAH, and so might, with more propriety, be rendered. The word is applied to Christ, Psalm 110:1, Colossians 3:16, and to the Holy Spirit, 2 Thessalonians 3:1. As a title of respect, it is applied to kings, Genesis 40:1, 2 Samuel 19:7, to princes and nobles, Genesis 42, Daniel 4:19, to a husband, Genesis 18:1, to a prophet, 1 Kings 18:1, 2 Kings 2:1, and to a respectable person, Genesis 24. Christ is called the Lord of glory, 1 Corinthians 2:8, and LORD of LORDS, Revelation 19:16. LORD, **verb transitive** To invest with the dignity and privileges of a lord. LORD, **verb intransitive** To domineer; to rule with arbitrary or despotic sway; sometimes followed by over, and sometimes by it, in the manner of a transitive verb.

H3119 *Day* יוֹמָם yômām *yo-mawm'* 51X **adverb, substantive S=** from H3117; daily:—daily, (by, in the) day(-time). **LG=** 1. By day, by day and by night, i.e. continually Leviticus 8:35, Numbers 9:21. 2. Daily, Ezekiel 1. **W=** DAY, **noun** 1. That part of the time of the earth's revolution on its axis, in which its surface is presented to the sun; the part of the twenty four hours when it is light; or the space of time between the rising and setting of the sun; In this sense, the day may commence at any period of the revolution. The Babylonians began the day at sun-rising; the Jews, at sun-setting; the Egyptians, at midnight, as do several nations in modern times, the British, French, Spanish, American, etc. This day in reference to civil transactions, is called the civil day Thus with us the day when a legal instrument is dated, begins and ends at midnight. 3. Light; sunshine. Romans 13:12. 4. Time specified; any period of time distinguished from other time; age; time with reference to the existence of a person or thing. Genesis 2:2. In this sense, the plural is often used; as, from the days of the judges; in the days of our fathers. In this sense also, the word is often equivalent to life, or earthly existence. 5. The contest of a day; battle; or day of combat. 6. An appointed or fixed time. 7. Time of commemorating an event; anniversary; the same day of the month, in any future year. We celebrate the day of our Savior's birth. "Days of grace," in theology,

Back it up

the time when mercy is offered to sinners. Psalm 95:7.

H3427 *Sits* יָשַׁב yāšaḇ *yaw-shab'* 1088x **verb S=** a primitive root; properly, to sit down (specifically as judge. in ambush, in quiet); by implication, to dwell, to remain; causatively, to settle, to marry:—(make to) abide(-ing), continue, (cause to, make to) dwell(-ing), ease self, endure, establish, × fail, habitation, haunt, (make to) inhabit(-ant), make to keep (house), lurking, × marry(-ing), (bring again to) place, remain, return, seat, set(-tle), (down-) sit(-down, still, -ting down, -ting (place) -uate), take, tarry. **LG=** 1. To sit, to sit down, Genesis 27:19. 2. To remain, abide Genesis 24:55. 3. To dwell, to dwell in, to inhabit, Genesis 13:6. 4. To be inhabited, as a place, city, country, Isaiah 13:20. **W=** SIT, **verb intransitive, preterit tense** sat. 1. To rest upon the buttocks, as animals; as, to sit on a sofa or on the ground. 2. To perch; to rest on the feet; as fowls. 3. To occupy a seat or place in an official capacity. The scribes and the Pharisees sit in Moses' seat. Matthew 23:2. 4. To be in a state of rest or idleness. Shall your brethren go to war, and shall ye sit here? Numbers 32:6. 5. To rest, lie or bear on, as a weight or burned; as, grief sits heavy on his heart. 6. To settle; to rest; to abide. 7. To incubate; to cover and warm eggs for hatching; as a fowl, Jeremiah 17:1. 8. To be adjusted; to be, with respect to fitness or unfitness; as, a coat sits well or ill. 9. To be placed in order to be painted; as, to sit for one's picture. 10. To be in any situation or condition. 11. To hold a session; to be officially engaged in public business; as judges, legislators or officers of any kind. 12. To exercise authority; as, to sit in judgment. 13. To be in any assembly or council as a member; to have a seat.

H3588 *For* כִּי kî *kee* 46x **conjunction S=** a primitive particle (the full form of the **prepositional prefix**) indicating causal relations of all kinds, antecedent or consequent; (by implication) very widely used as a relative **conjunction** or **adverb** (as below); often largely modified by other **particles** annexed:—and, (forasmuch, inasmuch, where-) as, assured(-ly), but, certainly, doubtless, else, even, except, for, how, (because, in, so, than) that, nevertheless, now, rightly, seeing, since, surely, then, therefore, (al-

Back it up

) though, till, truly, until, when, whether, while, whom, yea, yet. **LG=** 1. That we have. 2. So that, that, in order that, Job 6:11. 3. At that time, which, what time, when, Job 7:13. 4. Used of time, then, so. 5. As a **relative causal particle**: because, since, while. 6. After a negation, but, Genesis 24:3. 7. **Prepositions** turned into **conjunctions,** on account of, because, until that, until, for the reason that. **W=** FOR, **preposition** [The radical sense of for is to go, to pass, to advance, to reach or stretch.] 1. Against; in the place of; as a substitute or equivalent, noting equal value or satisfactory compensation, either in barter and sale, in contract, or in punishment, Genesis 48:17. 2. In the place of; instead of; noting substitution of persons, or agency of one in the place of another with equivalent authority. An attorney is empowered to act for his principal. 3. In exchange of; noting one thing taken or given in place of another; as, to quit the profession of law for that of a clergyman. 4. In the place of; instead of. 5. In the character of; noting resemblance; a sense derived from substitution or standing in the place of. 6. Towards; with the intention of

going to. 7. In advantage of; for the sake of; on account of; that is, towards, noting use, benefit or purpose 8. Conducive to; beneficial to; in favor of. 9. Leading or inducing to, as a motive. 10. Noting arrival, meeting, coming or possession. Wait patiently for an expected good. 11. Towards the obtaining of; in order to the arrival at or possession of. 12. Against; in opposition to; with a tendency to resist and destroy; as a remedy for the headache or toothache. 13. Against or on account of; in prevention of. 14. Because; on account of; by reason of. 15. With respect or regard to; on the part of. 16. Through a certain space; during a certain time; as, to travel for three days. 17. In quest of; in order to obtain; as, to search for arguments. 18. According to; as far as. 19. Noting meeting, coming together, or reception. I am ready for you. 20. Towards; of tendency to; as an inclination for food. 21. In favor of; on the part or side of; that is, towards or inclined to. 22. With a view to obtain; in order to possess. 23. Towards; with tendency to, or in favor of. 24. Notwithstanding; against; in opposition to. The fact may be so, for any thing that has yet

Dictionary, Lexicon & Strong's

appeared. 25. for the use of; to be used in; that is, towards, noting advantage. 26. In recompense of; in return of. Numbers 1:44. 27. In proportion to; or rather, looking towards, regarding. He is tall for his age. 28. By means of. 29. By the want of. 30. for my life or heart, though my life were to be given in exchange, or as the price of purchase. Numbers 1:44. 31. for to, denoting purpos, I came for to see you. FOR, conjunction 1. The word by which a reason is introduced of something before advanced, Matthew 5:45. In such sentences, for has the sense of because, by reason that, as in Numbers 14. 2. Because; on this account that; properly, for that.

H3605 *Whatsoever* כֹּל kōl *kole* 25X **masculine noun S=** from H3634; properly, the whole; hence, all, any or every (in the singular only, but often in a plural sense):—(in) all (manner, (ye)), altogether, any (manner), enough, every (one, place, thing), howsoever, as many as, (no-) thing, ought, whatsoever, (the) whole, whoso(-ever). **LG=** The whole, totality. 1. If used with regard to one continuous thing, the whole, Genesis 9:19. 2. When it refers to many things, many individuals, all, Isaiah 2:2. 3. Any,

whosoever, anything whatsoever, Ruth 4:7. 4. All, off all kinds, every sort, Levitius 19:23. 5. All, wholly, altogether, Psalm 39:6. **W=** WHATSOEVER, a compound of what, so, and ever, has the sense of whatever, and is less used than the latter. Indeed it is nearly obsolete.

H3651 *Therefore* כֵּן kēn *kane* 42X **adjective, adverb S=** from H3559; properly, set upright; hence (figuratively as adjective) just; but usually (as **adverb** or **conjunction**) rightly or so (in various applications to manner, time and relation; often with other particles):— after that (this, -ward, -wards), as... as, (for-) asmuch as yet, be (for which) cause, following, howbeit, in (the) like (manner, -wise), × the more, right, (even) so, state, straightway, such (thing), surely, there (where) -fore, this, thus, true, well, × you. **LG=** To lay up, upright, erect, metaphorically, honest. Genesis 42:11. 1. Rightly, well, 2 Kings 7:9. 2. So, thus, Genesis 1:7, 9, 11. 3. After that things have so occurred, i.e. afterwards. **W=** THEREFORE, adverb [there and for.] 1. For that; for that or this reason, referring to something previously stated. Luke 14:20.

2. Consequently. 3. In return or recompense for this or that.

H3808 *Not* לֹא *lō' lo* 76x **adverb**
S= a **primitive particle**; + not (the simple or abstract negation); by implication, no; often used with other **particles**:—× before, + or else, ere, + except, ig(-norant), much, less, nay, neither, never, no((-ne), -r, (-thing)), (× as though...,(can-), for) not (out of), of nought, otherwise, out of, + surely, + as truly as, + of a truth, + verily, for want, + whether, without.
LG= An **adverb** of negation, Psalm 16:10. 1. It is put absolutely when answering a question, no, Job 23:6 also in refusing, Genesis 19:2. 2. It stands as an interrogation when an affirmative answer is expected, Job 14:16. 3. It is put for without, 1 Chronicles 2:30. 4. Not yes, 2 Kings 20:4. 5. Psalm 43:1, Proverbs 30:25. **W=** NOT, **adverb** 1. A word that expreses negation, denial or refusal; as, he will no go; will you remain? I will not. 2. With the **substantive verb** in the following phrase, it denies being, or denotes extinction of existence, Job 7:1.

H3887 *Scornful* לוּץ *lûṣ loots*
27x **verb S=** a primitive root; properly, to make mouths at, i.e. to scoff; hence (from the effort to pronounce a foreign language) to interpret, or (generally) intercede:—ambassador, have in derision, interpreter, make a mock, mocker, scorn(-er, -ful), teacher. **LG=** To stammer, hence 1. To speak barbarously, i.e. in a foreign tongue, from those who speak a foreign language appearing, to those who are ignorant of it, as if they babbled and stammbered senselessly. 2. To deride, to mock anyone by imitating his voice in sport, Isaiah 28:10-11. Mocker, scoffer, i.e. a frivolous and impudent person, who despises scoffingly the most sacred precepts of religion, piety, and morals, Psalm 1:1, Proverbs 9:7-8. **W=** SCORN'FUL, **adjective** 1. Contemptuous; disdainful; entertaining scorn; insolent. 2. Acting in defiance or disregard. 3. In Scripture, holding religion in contempt; treating with disdain religion and the dispensations of God.

H3915 *Night* לַיִל *layil lah'-yil*
233x **masculine noun S=** from the same as H3883; properly, a twist (away of the light), i.e. night; figuratively, adversity:—(mid-) night (season). **LG=** Evening; obscurity. **W=** NIGHT, **noun** [The sense may be dark, black, or it

may be the decline of the day, from declining, departing.] 1. That part of the natural day when the sun is beneath the horizon, or the time from sunset to sunrise. 2. The time after the close of life; death. John 9:4. 3. A state of ignorance; intellectual and moral darkness; heathenish ignorance. Romans 13:12. 4. Adversity; a state of affliction and distress. Isaiah 21:4. 5. Obscurity; a state of concealment from the eye or the mind; unintelligibleness. Luke 12:20.

H4186 *Seat* מוֹשָׁב môšāḇ *mo-shawb'* 44x **masculine noun S=** from H3427; a seat; figuratively, a site; abstractly, a session; by extension an abode (the place or the time); by implication, population:—assembly, dwell in, dwelling(-place), wherein (that) dwelt (in), inhabited place, seat, sitting, situation, sojourning. **LG=** 1. A seat, place for sitting, 1 Samuel 20:18. 2. A sitting down, an assembly of persons, Psalm 1:1, 3. Habitation, Genesis 27:39, dwelling place, Leviticus 25:29, 4. The site (of a city), 2 Kings 2:19. **W=** SEAT, **noun** 1. That on which one sits; a chair, bench, stool or any other thing on which a person sits. Matthew 21:12. 2. The place

of sitting; throne; chair of state; tribunal; post of authority; as the seat of justice; judgment-seat. 3. Mansion; residence; dwelling; abode. 4. Site; situation. The seat of Eden has never been incontrovertibly ascertained.

5. That part of a saddle on which a person sits. 6. In horsemanship, posture or situation of a person on horseback. 7. A pew in a church; a place to sit in. 8. The place where a thing is settled or established. SEAT, **verb transitive** 1. To place on a seat; to cause to sit down. 2. To place in a post of authority, in office or a place of distinction. He seated his son in the professor's chair. 3. To settle; to fix in a particular place or country. 4. To fix; to set firm. 5. To place in a church; to assign seats to. 6. To appropriate the pews in, to particular families; as, to seat a church. 7. To repair by making the seat new; as, to seat a garment. SEAT, **verb intransitive** To rest; to lie down.

H4325 *Water* מַיִם mayim *mah'-yim* 1188x **masculine noun S=** dual of a **primitive noun** (but used in a singular sense); water; figuratively, juice; by euphemism, urine, semen:— piss, wasting,

Back it up

water(- ing, -course, -flood, -spring). **LG=** Water, Exodus 7:15, holy water, Numbers 5:17. Figuratively, juice of a hemlock or poppy, Jeremiah 8:14. A euphemism for urine, Ezekiel 47:4. Poetically water affords an image a) of abundance, Psalm 79:3, b) of great dangers, Psalm 18:17, c) of fear, Joshua 7:5, d) lasciviousness, Genesis 49:4.   **W=** WATER, **noun**
1. A fluid, the most abundant and most necessary for living beings of any in nature, except air. water when pure, is colorless, destitute of taste and smell, ponderous, transparent, and in a very small degree compressible. It is reposited in the earth in inexhaustible quantities, where it is preserved fresh and cool, and from which it issues in springs, which form streams and rivers. But the great reservoirs of water on the globe are the ocean, seas and lakes, which cover more than three fifths of its surface, and from which it is raised by evaporation, and uniting with the air in the state of vapor, is wafted over the earth, ready to be precipitated in the form of rain, snow or hail. WATER by the abstraction or loss of heat becomes solid, or in other words, is converted into

ice or snow; and by heat it is converted into steam, an elastic vapor, one of the most powerful agents in nature. Modern chemical experiments prove that water is a compound substance, consisting of a combination of oxygen and hydrogen gases, or rather the bases or ponderable matter of those gases; or about two volumes or measures of hydrogen gas and one of oxygen gas. The proportion of the ingredients in weight, is nearly 85 parts of oxygen to 15 of hydrogen. 2. The ocean; a sea; a lake; a river; any great collection of water; as in the phrases, to go by water to travel by water. 3. Urine; the animal liquor secreted by the kidneys and discharged from the bladder. 4. The color or luster of a diamond or pearl, sometimes perhaps of other precious stones; as a diamond of the first water that is, perfectly pure and transparent. 5. water is a name given to several liquid substances or humors in animal bodies; as the water of the pericardium, of dropsy, etc.

H4671 *Chaff* מֹץ mōṣ *motes* 8x **masculine noun S=** from H4160; chaff (as pressed out, i.e. winnowed or (rather) threshed loose):—chaff. **LG=** Zephaniah 2:2, chaff, husk, separated from the grain by winnowing, Isaiah 41:15, Psalm 1:4. **W=** CHAFF, **noun** 1. The husk, or dry calyx of corn, and grasses. In common language, the word is applied to the husks when separated from the corn by thrashing, riddling or winnowing. The word is sometimes used rather improperly to denote straw cut small for the food of cattle. 2. Refuse; worthless matter; especially that which is light, and apt to be driven by the wind. In scripture, false doctrines, fruitless designs, hypocrites and ungodly men are compared to chaff Psalm 1:4, Jeremiah 23:28, Isaiah 33:11, Matthew 3:12.

H4941 *Judgment* מִשְׁפָּט

mišpāṭ *mish-pawt'* 421X **masculine noun S=** from H8199; properly, a verdict (favorable or unfavorable) pronounced judicially, especially a sentence or formal decree (human or (participant's) divine law, individual or collective), including the act, the place, the suit, the crime, and the penalty; abstractly, justice, including a participant's right or privilege (statutory or customary), or even a style:— adversary, ceremony, charge, × crime, custom, desert, determination, discretion, disposing, due, fashion, form,

to be judged, judgment, just(-ice, -ly), (manner of) law(-ful), manner, measure, (due) order, ordinance, right, sentence, usest, × worthy, wrong. **LG=** 1. Judgment, Leviticus 19:15. 2. Right, that which is just, lawful, accoring to law. **W=** JUDG'MENT, **noun** The act of judging; the act or process of the mind in comparing its ideas, to find their agreement or disagreement, and to ascertain truth; or the process of examining facts and arguments, to ascertain propriety and justice; or the process of examining the relations between one proposition and another. 1. The faculty of the mind by which man is enabled to compare ideas and ascertain the relations of terms and propositions; as a man of clear judgment or sound judgment The judgment may be biased by prejudice. Judgment supplies the want of certain knowledge. 2. The determination of the mind, formed from comparing the relations of ideas, or the comparison of facts and arguments. In the formation of our judgments, we should be careful to weigh and compare all the facts connected with the subject. 3. In law, the sentence of doom pronounced in any cause, civil or criminal, by the judge or court by which it is tried. Judgment may be rendered on demurrer, on a verdict, on a confession or default, or on a non-suit. Judgment though pronounced by the judge or court, is properly the determination or sentence of the law. A pardon may be pleaded in arrest of judgment. 4. The right or power of passing sentence. 5. Determination; decision. 6. Opinion; notion. 7. In Scripture, the spirit of wisdom and prudence, enabling a person to discern right and wrong, good and evil. Psalm 72:2. 8. A remarkable punishment; an extraordinary calamity inflicted by God on sinners. Proverbs 19:28. Isaiah 26:8. 9. The spiritual government of the world. The Father hath committed all judgment to the Son. John 5:22. 10. The righteous statutes and commandments of God are called his judgments. Psalm 119:66. 11. The doctrines of the gospel, or God's word. Matthew 12:18. 12. Justice and equity. Luke 11:31. Isaiah 1:17. 13. The decrees and purposes of God concerning nations. Romans 11:33. 14. A court or tribunal. Matthew 5:21. 15. Controversies, or decisions of controversies. 1 Corinthians 6:4

16. The gospel, or kingdom of grace. Matthew 12:18. 17. The final trial of the human race, when God will decide the fate of every individual, and award sentence according to justice. "For God shall bring every work into judgment with every secret thing, whether it be good, or whether it be evil." Ecclesiastes 12:14.

H5034 *Wither* נָבֵל *nābēl naw-bale* 25x **verb S=** A primitive root; to wilt; generally, to fall away, fail, faint; figuratively, to be foolish or (morally) wicked; causatively, to despise, disgrace:—disgrace, dishonor, lightly esteem, fade (away, -ing), fall (down, -ling, off), do foolishly, come to nought, × surely, make vile, wither. **LG=** 1. To be, or to become withered, faded, used of leaves and flowers falling off from being faded, Psalm 1:3. 2. Figuratively applied to men, to fall down, to faint, to lose one's strength, Psalm 18:46. 3. To be foolish, to act foolishly, (withering and decay being applied to folly and impiety, just as on the contrary, strength is applied to virtue and piety, Proverbs 30:32. **W=** WITHER, **verb intransitive** 1. To fade; to lose its native freshness; to become sapless; to dry. Ezekiel 17:9. 2. To waste; to pine away; as animal bodies; as a withered hand. Matthew 12:10. 3. To lose or want animal moisture. WITHER, **verb transitive** 1. To cause to fade and become dry; as, the sun withereth the grass. James 1:11. 2. To cause to shrink, wrinkle and decay, for want of animal moisture.

H5086 *Drives away* נָדַף nādap̄ *naw-daf'* 9x **verb S=** a primitive root; to shove asunder, i.e. disperse:— drive (away, to and fro), thrust down, shaken, tossed to and fro. **LG=** To dispel, to drive away, as the wind drives away chaff, stubble, smoke. Psalm 68:3. To put to flight an enemy, i.e. to conquer, metaphorically Job 32:13. **W=** DRIVE, **verb transitive preterit tense** Drove, [formerly drave; **participle passive** Driven] 1. To impel or urge forward by force; to force; to move by physical force. 2. To compel or urge forward by other means than absolute physical force, or by means that compel the will; as, to drive cattle to market. 3. To chase; to hunt. 4. To impel a team of horses or oxen to move forward, and to direct their course; hence, to guide or regulate the course of the carriage drawn by them. 5. To impel to greater speed. 6. To clear any place by forcing away what is in it. 7. To force; to

compel; in a general sense. 8. To hurry on inconsiderately; often with *on*. In this sense it is more generally **intransitive**. 9. To distress; to straighten; as desperate men far driven. 10. To impel by influence of passion. 11. To urge; to press; as, to drive an argument. 12. To impel by moral influence; to compel; as, the reasoning of his opponent drove him to acknowledge his error. 13. To carry on; to prosecute; to keep in motion; as, to drive a trade; to drive business. 14. To make light by motion or agitation; as, to drive feathers. To drive away, to force to remove to a distance; to expel; to dispel; to scatter. To drive off, to compel to remove from a place; to expel; to drive to a distance. To drive out, to expel. DRIVE, **verb intransitive** 1. To be forced along; to be impelled; to be moved by any physical force or agent; as, a ship drives before the wind. 2. To rush and press with violence; as, a storm drives against the house. 3. To pass in a carriage; as, he drove to London. 4. To aim at or tend to; to urge towards a point; to make an effort to reach or obtain; as, we know the end the author is driving at. 5. To aim a blow; to strike at with force. DRIVE, in all its senses, implies forcible or violent action. It is opposed to lead. To drive a body is to move it by applying a force behind; to lead is to cause to move by applying the force before, or forward of the body.

H5414 *Brings forth* נָתַן nāṯan *naw-than'* 2008x **verb S=** a primitive root; to give, used with greatest latitude of application (put, make, etc.):—add, apply, appoint, ascribe, assign, × avenge, × be (healed), bestow, bring (forth, hither), cast, cause, charge, come, commit, consider, count, cry, deliver (up), direct, distribute, do, × doubtless, × without fail, fasten, frame, × get, give (forth, over, up), grant, hang (up), × have, × indeed, lay (unto charge, up), (give) leave, lend, let (out), lie, lift up, make, O that, occupy, offer, ordain, pay, perform, place, pour, print, × pull, put (forth), recompense, render, requite, restore, send (out), set (forth), shew, shoot forth (up), sing, slander, strike, (sub-) mit, suffer, × surely, × take, thrust, trade, turn, utter, weep, willingly, withdraw, would (to) God, yield. **LG=** 1. To give, Genesis 25:6. 2. To set, to put, to place, Genesis 1:17. 3. To make, Leviticus 19:28. **W=** BRING, **verb transitive** 1. To fetch; to bear,

convey or lead from a distant to a nearer place, or to a person; as, bring me a book from the shelf; bring me a morsel of bread. In this sense, it is opposed to carry, and it is applied to the person bearing or leading, in opposition to sending or transmitting by another. 2. To produce; to procure as a cause; to draw to. 3. To attract or draw along. 4. To cause to come; to cause to proceed from a distant place, in company, or at the same time; as, to bring a boat over a river; to bring a horse or carriage; to bring a cargo of dry goods. 5. To cause to come to a point, by moral influence; used of the mind, and implying previous remoteness, aversion, alienation, or disagreement; as, to bring the mind to assent to a proposition; or to bring a man to terms, by persuasion or argument. In this sense, it is nearly equivalent to persuade, prevail upon, or induce. The same process is effected by custom, and other causes. Habit brings us to relish things at first disagreeable; reflection brings a man to his senses, and whether the process is slow or rapid, the sense of the **verb** is the same. To bring to the mind any thing before and forgotten, is to recall; but the sense of bring is the same. The primary sense is to lead, draw or cause to come; the sense of conveying or bearing is secondary. The use of this **verb** is so extensive, and incorporated into so many peculiar phrases, that it is not easy to reduce its significations within any precise limits. In general, the verb bring implies motion from a place remote, either in a literal or figurative sense. It is used with various modifying words.bring back is to recall, implying previous departure, either in a literal or figurative sense.

H5712 *Congregation* עֵדָה
'ēḏâ *ay-daw'* 149x **feminine noun**
S= feminine of H5707 in the original sense of fixture; a stated assemblage (specifically, a concourse, or generally, a family or crowd):—assembly, company, congregation, multitude, people, swarm. Compare H5713.
LG= An appointed meeting, an assembly. 1. The congregation of the Israelites, Exodus 12:3. 2. A private domestic meeting, a family, Job 16:7. In a bad sense, a crowd (of wicked men), Numbers 16:5, Psalm 22:17. 3. a swarm (of bees) Judges 14:8. **W=** CONGREGATION, **noun** 1. The act of bringing together,

or assembling. 2. A collection or assemblage of separate things; as a congregation of vapors. 3. More generally, an assembly or persons; and appropriately, an assembly of persons met for the worship of God, and for religious instruction. 4. An assembly of rulers. Numbers 35:12. 5. An academical assembly for transacting business of the university.

H5921 *By* עַל 'al *al* 48x
conjunction, preposition S= properly, the same as H5920 used as a **preposition** (in the singular or plural often with prefix, or as **conjunction** with a **particle** following); above, over, upon, or against (yet always in this last relation with a downward aspect) in a great variety of applications:— above, according to(-ly), after, (as) against, among, and, × as, at, because of, beside (the rest of), between, beyond the time, × both and, by (reason of), × had the charge of, concerning for, in (that), (forth, out) of, (from) (off), (up-) on, over, than, through(-out), to, touching, × with. **LG=** 1. Super, upon, when anything is put on the upper part of another, so as to stand or lie upon it, or have it for its substatum. 2. With the idea of impending, being high, being

Back it up

suspended over anything, without, however, touching it, above, over. 3. The sense of neighborhood and contiguity, at, by, near, being high over, i.e. Numbers 24:6. 4. Denotes motion (especially when rapid, unto or towards any place. **W=** BY, preposition 1. Near; close; as, sit by me. 2. Near, in motion; as, to move, go or pass by a church. But it seems, in other phrases, or with a **verb** in the past time, to signify past, gone beyond. "The procession is gone by. 3. Through, or with, denoting the agent, means, instrument or cause; as, "a city is destroyed by fire." 4. "Day by day," denotes passing from one to another, or each particular separately taken. 5. "By the space of seven years," denotes through, passing or continuing, during. 6. "By this time, the sun had risen." denotes, at, present or come to. 7. According to; as, "this appears by his own account;" "these are good rules to live by." 8. On; as, "to pass by land or water." 9. It is placed before words denoting quantity, measure or proportion; as, to sell by the pound. 10. It is used to represent the means or instrument of swearing, or affirming; as, to swear by heaven, or by earth; to affirm by all that is sacred. 11. In the phrase, "he has a Bible by him" by denotes nearness or presence. 12. "To sit by one"s self" is to sit alone, or without company. 13. "To be present by attorney." denotes means or instrument; through or in the presence of a substitute. 14. In the phrase, "North by West, " the sense seems to be north passing to the west, inclining or going westward, or near west.

H5929 *Leaf* עָלֶה ʻālê *aw-leh'* 18x **masculine noun S=** from H5927; a leaf (as coming up on a tree); collectively, foliage:—branch, leaf. **LG=** Leaf, Genesis 3:7, the sense of growing and sprouting forth. **W=** LEAF, **noun** plural leaves 1. In botany, leaves are organs of perspiration and inhalation in plants. 2. The thin, extended part of a flower; a petal. 3. A part of a book containing two pages. 4. The side of a double door. 1 Kings 6:1. 5. Something resembling a leaf in thinness and extension; a very thin plate; as gold leaf. 6. The movable side of a table. LEAF, **verb intransitive** To shoot out leaves; to produce leaves. "The trees leaf in May."

H5975 *Stands* עָמַד ʻāmaḏ *aw-mad'* 521x **verb S=** a primitive root;

to stand, in various relations (literal and figurative, intransitive and transitive):—abide (behind), appoint, arise, cease, confirm, continue, dwell, be employed, endure, establish, leave, make, ordain, be (over), place, (be) present (self), raise up, remain, repair, serve, set (forth, over, -tle, up), (make to, make to be at a, with-) stand (by, fast, firm, still, up), (be at a) stay (up), tarry. **LG=** 1. To stand, to set firmly, to sustain, used of men, Genesis 24:30. 2. To stand for, to stand firm, to remain, to endure, Psalm 33:11. 3. To stand still, to stop, 1 Samuel 20:38. 4. To stand up, arise, Daniel 12:1. 5. To be constituted, set, appointed, Ezra 10:14. **W=** STAND, **verb intransitive preterit tense** and **participle passive** stood. 1. To be upon the feet, as an animal; not to sit, kneel or lie. 1 Kings 8:11. 2. To be erect, supported by the roots, as a tree or other plant. 3. To be on its foundation; not to be overthrown or demolished. 4. To be placed or situated; to have a certain position or location. 5. To remain upright, in a moral sense; not to fall. 6. To become erect. 7. To stop; to halt; not to proceed. 8. To stop; to be at a stationary point. 9. To be in a state of fixedness; hence, to continue; to endure. 10. To be fixed or steady; not to vacillate. 11. To be in or to maintain a posture of resistance or defense. Esther 8:11. 12. To be placed with regard to order or rank. 13. To be in particular state; to be, emphatically expressed, that is, to be fixed or set. 14. To continue unchanged or valid; not to fail or become void. Psalm 89:28. 15. To consist; to have its being and essence. Hebrews 9:1. 16. To have a place. 17. To be in any state. 18. To be in particular respect or relation; as, to stand godfather to one. 19. To be, with regard to state of mind. Psalm 4:4. 20. To succeed; to maintain ones ground; not to fail; to be acquitted; to be safe. 21. To hold a course at sea; as, to stand from the shore. 22. To have a direction. 23. To offer ones self as a candidate. "He stood to be elected one of the proctors of the university." 24. To place ones self; to be placed. Deuteronomy 5:31. 25. To stagnate; not to flow. 26. To be satisfied or convinced. 27. To make delay. "I cannot stand to examine every particular." 28. To persist; to persevere. 29. To adhere; to abide. 30. To be permanent; to endure; not to vanish or fade; as, the color will stand. To stand by, 1. To be near; to be a spectator; to be present. 2. To be aside; to be placed aside with disregard. 3. To maintain; to defend; to support; not to desert. 4. To rest on for support; to be supported.To stand for, 1. To offer ones self as a candidate. 2. To side with; to support; to maintain, or to profess or attempt to maintain. 3. To be in the place of; to be the substitute or representative of. 4. In seamens language, to direct the course towards. To stand off, 1. To keep at a distance. 2. Not to comply. 3. To keep at a distance in friendship or social intercourse; to forbear intimacy. 4. To appear prominent; to have relief. To stand out, 1. To project; to be prominent. Psalm 73. 2. To persist in opposition or resistance; not to yield or comply; not to give way or recede. 3. With seamen, to direct the course from land or a harbor. To stand to, 1. To ply; to urge efforts; to persevere. 2. To remain fixed in a purpose or opinion. 3. To abide by; to adhere; as to a contract, assertion, promise, etc.; as, to stand to an award; to stand to ones word. 4. Not to yield; not to fly; to maintain the ground. To stand up, 1. To rise from sitting; to be on the feet. 2. To arise in

order to gain notice. 3. To make a party. To stand up for, to defend; to justify; to support, or attempt to support; as, to stand up for the administration. To stand upon, 1. To concern; to interest. 2. To value; to pride. 3. To insist; as, to stand upon security. To stand with, to be consistent. The faithful servants of God will receive what they pray for, so far as stands with his purposes and glory. To stand against, to oppose; to resist. To stand fast, to be fixed; to be unshaken or immovable. To stand in hand, to be important to ones interest.STAND, **verb transitive** 1. To endure; to sustain; to bear. 2. To endure; to resist without yielding or receding. 3. To await; to suffer; to abide by. To stand ones ground, to deep the ground or station one has taken; to maintain ones position. To stand it, to bear; to be able to endure; or to maintain ones ground or state. To stand trial, is to sustain the trial or examination of a cause; not to give up without trial. STAND, **noun** 1. A stop; a halt; as, to make a stand; to come to a stand either in walking or in any progressive business. 2. A station; a place or post where one stands; or a place convenient for persons to remain for any

Dictionary, Lexicon & Strong's

purpose. The sellers of fruit have their several stands in the market. 3. Rank; post; station. 4. The act of opposing. 5. The highest point; or the ultimate point of progression, where a stop is made, and regressive motion commences. 6. A young tree, usually reserved when the other trees are cut. 7. A small table; as a candle-stand. 8. In commerce, a weight of from two hundred and a half to three hundred of pitch. 9. Something on which a thing rests or is laid; as a hay-stand.

H6086 *Tree* עֵץ ʿēṣ *ates* 328x **masculine noun S=** from H6095; a tree (from its firmness); hence, wood (plural sticks):— carpenter, gallows, helve, pine, plank, staff, stalk, stick, stock, timber, tree, wood. **LG=** 1. A tree. 2. Wood, specially of a wooden post, stake, gibbet, Genesis 40:19. **W=** TREE, **noun** 1. The general name of the largest of the vegetable kind, consisting of a firm woody stem springing from woody roots, and spreading above into branches which terminate in leaves. A tree differs from a shrub principally in size, many species of trees growing to the highth of fifty or sixty feet, and some species to seventy or eighty, and a

few, particularly the pine, to a much greater height Trees are of various kinds; as nuciferous, or nut-bearing trees; bacciferous, or berry-bearing; coniferous, or cone-bearing, etc. Some are forest-trees, and useful for timber or fuel; others are fruit trees, and cultivated in gardens and orchards; others are used chiefly for shade and ornament. 2. Something resembling a tree consisting of a stem or stalk and branches; as a genealogical tree. 3. In ship-building, pieces of timber are called chess-trees, cross-trees, roof-trees, tressel-trees, etc. 4. In Scripture, a cross, Acts 10:39. 5. Wood.

H6098 *Counsel* עֵצָה ʿēṣâ *ay-tsaw'* 88x **feminine noun S=** from H3289; advice; by implication, plan; also prudence:—advice, advisement, counsel(-lor), purpose. **LG=** 1. Counsel which anyon gives or receives, 2 Samuel 16:20. 2. Counsel which anyone forms, Isaiah 19:3, to execute a plan or counsel, Isaiah 30:1. Especially used of the counsel or purpose of God, Job 38:2. counsel as the faculty of forming plans, i.e. prudence, wisdom, especially that of God, Isaiah 11:2. **W=** COUNSEL, **noun**

to consult; to ask, to assail.
1. Advice; opinion, or instruction, given upon request or otherwise, for directing the judgment or conduct of another; opinion given upon deliberation or consultation, Proverbs 20:5, 2 Chronicles 25:16.
2. Consultation; interchange of opinions. Psalm 55:14.
3. Deliberation; examination of consequences. 4. Prudence; deliberate opinion or judgment, or the faculty or habit of judging with caution. Ezekiel 7:26. 5. In a bad sense, evil advice or designs; art; machination. Job 5:13.
6. Secresy; the secrets entrusted in consultation; secret opinions or purposes. 7. In a scriptural sense, purpose; design; will; decree. Acts 4:28. 8. Directions of Gods word. Psalm 73:24.
9. The will of God or his truth and doctrines concerning the way of salvation. Acts 20:27. 10. Those who give counsel in law; any counselor or advocate, or any number of counselor. COUNSEL, **verb transitive** 1. To give advice or deliberate opinion to another for the government of his conduct; to advise. Revelations 3. 2. To exhort, warn, admonish, or instruct. We ought frequently to counsel our children against the vices

of the age. They that will not be counseled, cannot be helped.

H6213 *Does* עָשָׂה ʿāśâ *aw-saw'* 2633x **verb S=** a primitive root; to do or make, in the broadest sense and widest application:— accomplish, advance, appoint, apt, be at, become, bear, bestow, bring forth, bruise, be busy, × certainly, have the charge of, commit, deal (with), deck, displease, do, (ready) dress(-ed), (put in) execute(-ion), exercise, fashion, feast, (fight-) ing man, finish, fit, fly, follow, fulfill, furnish, gather, get, go about, govern, grant, great, hinder, hold (a feast), × indeed, be industrious, journey, keep, labour, maintain, make, be meet, observe, be occupied, offer, officer, pare, bring (come) to pass, perform, pracise, prepare, procure, provide, put, requite, × sacrifice, serve, set, shew, × sin, spend, × surely, take, × thoroughly, trim, × very, vex, be (warr-) ior, work(-man), yield, use. **LG=** 1 To labor, to work about anything, Exodus 5:9. 2. To make, to produce by labor. **W=** DOES, the third person of the **verb** do, **indicative mode**, **present tense,** contracted from doeth. DO, **verb transitive** or **auxiliary; preterit tense** Did; **participle passive** Done, pronounced dun. 1. To perform;

to execute; to carry into effect; to exert labor or power for brining any thing to the state desired, or to completion; or to bring any thing to pass. Exodus 20:9. 2. To practice; to perform; as, to do good or evil. 3. To perform for the benefit or injury of another; with for or to; for, when the thing is beneficial; to, in either case. 1 Samuel 22:3. 4. To execute; to discharge; to convey; as, do a message to the king. 5. To perform; to practice; to observe. 1 John 1:1. 6. To exert. 2 Timothy 4:5. 7. To transact; as, to do business with another. 8. To finish; to execute or transact and bring to a conclusion. The sense of completion is often implie. 9. To perform in an exigency; to have recourse to, as a consequential or last effort; to take a step or measure. Isaiah 10:3. 10. To make or cause. 11. To put. 12. To answer the purpose. 2 Samuel 16:10. To do with, to dispose of; to make use of; to employ. Also, to have concern with; to have business; to deal. To do away, to remove; to destroy; as, to do away imperfections; to do away prejudices. DO, **verb intransitive** 1. To act or behave, in any manner, well or ill; to conduct ones self. 2 Kings 17:12. 2. To fare; to be in a state with regard to

sickness or health. 3. To succeed; to accomplish a purpose.

H6256 *Season* עֵת ʻēt *ayth* 296x **feminine noun S=** from H5703; time, especially (**adverb** with **preposition**) now, when, etc.:— after, (al-) ways, × certain, continually, evening, long, (due) season, so (long) as, (even-, evening-, noon-) tide, (meal-), what) time, when. **LG=** Time, a fit or proper time, in its time, Proverbs 15:23, a certain time, at this time, now, every time, every season, Psalm 10:5, at the time of evening, Genesis 8:11. **W=** SE'ASON. **noun** Season literally signifies that which comes or arrives; and in this general sense, is synonymous with time. Hence, 1. A fit or suitable time; the convenient time; the usual or appointed time; as, the messenger arrived in season; in good season. 2. Any time, as distinguished from others. 3. A time of some continuance, but not long. Acts 13:11. 4. One of the four divisions of the year, spring, summer, autumn, winter. 5. That which matures or prepares for the taste; that which gives a relish. SE'ASON, **verb transitive** 1. To render palatable, or to give a higher relish to, by the addition or mixture of another substance more

B a c k i t u p

pungent or pleasant; as, to season meat with salt. Leviticus 2:13. 2. To render more agreeable, pleasant or delightful; to give relish or zest to by something that excites, animates or exhilarates. 3. To render more agreeable, or less rigorous and severe; to temper; to moderate; to qualify by admixture. 4. To imbue; to tinge or taint. 5. To fit any use by time or habit; to mature; to prepare. 6. To prepare for use by drying or hardening; to take out or suffer to escape the natural juices; as, to season timber. 7. To prepare or mature for a climate; to accustom to and enable to endure; as, to season the body to a particular climate. SE'ASON, **verb intransitive** 1. To become mature; to grow fit for use; to become adapted to a climate, as the human body. 2. To become dry and hard by the escape of natural juices, or by being penetrated with other substances. Timber seasons well under cover in the air, and ship timber seasons in salt water. 3. To betoken; to savor.

H6388 *Rivers* פֶּלֶג peleḡ *peh'-leg* 10x **masculine noun S=** from H6385; a rill (i.e. small channel of water, as in irrigation):—river, stream. **LG=** 1. A stream, a river, a channel, watercourse, so

called from the idea of dividing, Job 38:25. Flowing, fluctuating, bubbling up, used of streams of tears, Lamentations 3:48. **W=** RIV'ER, **noun** 1. A large stream of water flowing in a channel on land towards the ocean, a lake or another river. It is larger than a rivulet or brook; but is applied to any stream from the size of a mill-stream to that of the Danube, Maranon and Mississippi. We give this name to large streams which admit the tide and mingle salt water with fresh, as the rivers Hudson, Delaware and St. Lawrence. 2. A large stream; copious flow; abundance; as rivers of blood; rivers of oil.

H6529 *Fruit* פְּרִי pᵊrî *per-ee'* 119x **masculine noun S=** from H6509; fruit (literally or figuratively):—bough, (first-)fruit(-ful), reward. **LG=** 1. Fruit, whether of the earth and field, Genesis 4:3, or of a tree, Genesis 1:12. Metaphorically, used of the result of labor or endeavor, the image often being preserved, Isaiah 3:10. 2. offsping, Lamentations 2:20. **W=** FRUIT, noun 1. In a general sense, whatever the earth produces for the nourishment of animals, or for clothing or profit. Among the fruits of the earth are included not only corn of all kinds, but grass, cotton, flax, grapes and all cultivated plants. 2. In a more limited sense, the produce of a tree or other plant; the last production for the propagation or multiplication of its kind; the seed of plants, or the part that contains the seeds; as wheat, rye, oats, apples, quinces, pears, cherries, acorns, melons, etc. 3. In botany, the seed of a plant, or the seed with the pericarp. 4. Production; that which is produced. Ephesians 5:9. 5. The produce of animals; offspring; young; as the fruit of the womb, of the loins, of the body. 6. Effect or consequence. Isaiah 3:10. 7. Advantage; profit; good derived. Romans 6:21. 8. Production, effect or consequence; in an ill sense; as the fruits of sin; the fruits of intemperance.

H6662 *Righteous* צַדִּיק

ṣadîq *tsad-deek'* 206x **adjective S=** from H6663; just:—just, lawful, righteous (man). **LG=** 1. Just, righteous, used of a judge or king, who maintains the right and dispenses justice, 2 Samuel 23:3, hence used very often of God as being a just judge, Deuteronomy 32:4, both in punishing 2 Chronicles 12:6, and in rewarding, Psalm 112:6. 2. One

who has a just cause, Exodus 9:27. 3. Of a private person, just towards other men, Proverbs 29:7, obedient to the laws of God, hence upright, honest, virtuous, pious. **W=** RIGHTEOUS, **adjective** 1. Just; accordant to the divine law. Applied to persons, it denotes one who is holy in heart, and observant of the divine commands in practice; as a righteous man. Applied to things, it denotes consonant to the divine will or to justice; as a righteous act. It is used chiefly in theology, and applied to God, to his testimonies and to his saints. The righteous in Scripture, denote the servants of God, the saints. 2. Just; equitable; merited.

H6743 *Prosper* צָלַח ṣālēaḥ

tsaw-lakh' 65x **verb S=** a primitive root; to push forward, in various senses (literal or figurative, transitive or intransitive):—break out, come (mightily), go over, be good, be meet, be profitable, (cause to, effect, make to, send) prosper(-ity, -ous, -ously). **LG=** 1. To go over or through (as a river), 2 Samuel 19:18. 2. To attack, to fall upon, used of the Spirit of Jehovah falling upon a man, Judges 14:19. 3. To go on well, to prosper, to succeed, Isaiah 53:10.

W= PROS'PER, **verb transitive** To favor; to render successful. PROS'PER, **verb intransitive** To be successful; to succeed. Genesis 39:3. 1. To grow or increase; to thrive; to make gain; as, to prosper in business.

H6965 *Stand* קוּם *qûm* *koom* 628x **verb S=** a primitive root; to rise (in various applications, literal, figurative, intensive and causative):—abide, accomplish, × be clearer, confirm, continue, decree, × be dim, endure, × enemy, enjoin, get up, make good, help, hold, (help to) lift up (again), make, × but newly, ordain, perform, pitch, raise (up), rear (up), remain, (a-) rise (up) (again, against), rouse up, set (up), (e-) stablish, (make to) stand (up), stir up, strengthen, succeed, (as-, make) sure(-ly), (be) up(-hold, -rising). **LG=** 1. To arise, from a seat, from bed, Genesis 19:1, 2. To stand before anyone, to oppose him, Joshua 7:13, to stand fast, to remain, to continue, Job 15:29. 3. To live. **W=** See H5975.

H7307 *Wind* רוּחַ *rûaḥ* *roo'-akh* 378x **feminine noun S=** from H7306; wind; by resemblance breath, i.e. a sensible (or even violent) exhalation; figuratively, life, anger, unsubstantiality; by extension, a region of the sky; by resemblance spirit, but only of a rational being (including its expression and functions):— air, anger, blast, breath, × cool, courage, mind, × quarter, × side, spirit(-ual), tempest, × vain, (whirl-) wind(-y). **LG=** 1. Spirit, breath, breath of the mouth, Psalm 33:6, Isaiah 11:4. Used of anything quickly perishing, Job 7:7. Breath of the nostrils, snuffing, snorting, Job 4:9, Psalm 18:16, hence anger. Breath of air, air in motion, i.e. breeze, Job 41:8. 2. Breath, life, the vital principle, which shows itself in the breathing of the mouth and nostrils, whether of men or of beasts, Ecclesiastes 3:21. 3. The rational mind or spirit, as the seat of the senses, affections, and emotions of various kinds, Proverbs 25:28. **W=** WIND, **noun** The primary sense is to move, flow, rush or drive along. 1. Air in motion with any degree of velocity, indefinitely; a current of air. When the air moves moderately, we call it a light wind or a breeze; when with more velocity, we call it a fresh breeze, and when with violence, we call it a gale, storm or tempest. Winds are denominated from the point of compass from which they blow; as a north wind;

Back it up

an east wind; a south wind; a west wind; a southwest wind etc. 2. The four winds, the cardinal points of the heavens. Ezekiel 37:9. 3. Direction of the wind from other points of the compass than the cardinal, or any point of compass. 4. Breath; power of respiration. 5. Air in motion form any force or action. 6. Breath modulated by the organs or by an instrument. 7. Air impregnated with scent. 8. Any thing insignificant or light as wind. 9. Flatulence; air generated in the stomach and bowel.

H7563 *Ungodly* רָשָׁע rāšāʿ *raw-shaw'* 263x **adjective S=** from H7561; morally wrong; concretely, an (actively) bad person:— condemned, guilty, ungodly, wicked (man), that did wrong. **LG=** 1. Wicked, unrighteous, Genesis 18:23. 2. Having an unrighteous cause, Exodus 23:7, 3. Guilty, liable to punishment, Genesis 18:23. Guilty of death, Numbers 35:31. **W=** UNGOD'LY, **adjective** 1. Wicked; impious; neglecting the fear and worship of God, or violating his commands. 1 Peter 4:18. 2. Sinful; contrary to the divine commands; as ungodly deeds. Jude 1:4. 3. Polluted by wickedness; as an ungodly day.

H8362 *Planted* שָׁתַל *šāṯal shaw-thal'* 10x **verb S=** a primitive root; to transplant:—plant. **LG=** To plant, a poetic word, Psalm 1:3, 92:14. **W=** PLANT'ED, **participle passive** Set in the earth for propagation; set; fixed; introduced; established. 1. Furnished with seeds or plants for growth; as a planted field. 2. Furnished with the first inhabitants; settled; as territory planted with colonists. 3. Filled or furnished with what is new.

H8451 *Law* תּוֹרָה *tôrâ to-raw'* 219x **feminine noun S=** from H3384; a precept or statute, especially the Decalogue or Pentateuch:— law. **LG=** 1. Instruction, doctrin, Job 22:22, human instruction, as that of parents, Proverbs 1:8, or divine through prophets, Isaiah 1:10. 2. Law, human manner and principles which men follow, 2 Samuel 7:19, or divine e.g. the law of sacrifice, Leviticus 6:7, or collective laws, the book of the law, Joshua 1:8, Exodus 18:20, Leviticus 26:46. **W=** LAW, **noun** A law is that which is laid, set or fixed, like statute, constitution, from Latin statuo. 1. A rule, particularly an established or permanent rule, prescribed by the supreme power of a state to its subjects, for regulating their actions, particularly their social actions. Laws are imperative or mandatory, commanding what shall be done; prohibitory, restraining from what is to be forborn; or permissive, declaring what may be done without incurring a penalty. The laws which enjoin the duties of piety and morality, are prescribed by God and found in the Scriptures. 2. Municipal law is a rule of civil conduct prescribed by the supreme power of a state, commanding what its subjects are to do, and prohibiting what they are to forbear; a statute. 3. Law of nature, is a rule of conduct arising out of the natural relations of human beings established by the Creator, and existing prior to any positive precept. Thus it is a law of nature, that one man should not injure another, and murder and fraud would be crimes, independent of any prohibition from a supreme power. 4. Laws of animal nature, the inherent principles by which the economy and functions of animal bodies are performed, such as respiration, the circulation of the blood, digestion, nutrition, various secretions, etc. 5. Laws of vegetation, the principles by which plants are produced, and their growth carried on till they arrive to perfection. 6. Physical laws, or laws of nature. 7. Laws of nations, the rules that regulate the mutual intercourse of nations or states. 8. Moral law a law which prescribes to men their religious and social duties, in other words, their duties to God and to each other. The immoral law is summarily contained in the Decalogue or ten commandments, written by the finger of God on two tables of stone, and delivered to Moses on mount Sinai. Exodus 20:1. 9. Ecclesiastical law a rule of action prescribed for the government of a church; otherwise called Canon law. 10. Written law a law or rule of action prescribed or enacted by a sovereign, and promulgated and recorded in writing; a written statute, ordinance, edict or decree. 11. Unwritten or common law a rule of action which derives its authority from long usage, or established custom, which has been immemorially received and recognized by judicial tribunals. 12. By-law, a law of a city, town or private corporation. 13. Mosaic law the institutions of Moses, or

Dictionary, Lexicon & Strong's

the code of laws prescribed to the Jews, as distinguished from the gospel. 14. Ceremonial law the Mosaic institutions which prescribe the external rites and ceremonies to be observed by the Jews, as distinct from the moral precepts, which are of perpetual obligation. 15. A rule of direction; a directory; as reason and natural conscience. Romans 2:12. 16. That which governs or has a tendency to rule; that which has the power of controlling. Romans 7:1. 17. The word of God; the doctrines and precepts of God, or his revealed will. Psalm 1:2. 18. The Old Testament. John 10:34. 19. The institutions of Moses, as distinct from the other parts of the Old Testament; as the law and the prophets. 20. A rule or axiom of science or art; settled principle; as the laws of versification or poetry. 21. Law martial, or the rules ordained for the government of an army or military force. 22. Marine laws, rules for the regulation of navigation, and the commercial intercourse of nations. 23. Commercial law law-merchant, the system of rules by which trade and commercial intercourse are regulated between merchants. 24. Judicial process; prosecution of right in courts of law. 25. Jurisprudence; as in the title, Doctor of Laws. 26. In general, law is a rule of action prescribed for the government of rational beings or moral agents, to which rule they are bound to yield obedience, in default of which they are exposed to punishment; or law is a settled mode or course of action or operation in irrational beings and in inanimate bodies.

_____

_____

_____

_____

_____

_____

_____

_____

_____

_____

_____

_____

_____

_____

RenewingLives.com

Back it up

Ethelbert William Bullinger (December 15, 1837—June 6, 1913)

E.W. Bullinger was an Anglican clergyman (for over thirty years), Biblical scholar with a Doctor of Divinity degree, composer, singer, theologian, and writer.

At the age of twenty-three, he married Emma Dobson (thirteen years his senior), with whom he had two sons.

He held the position of clerical secretary of the Trinitarian Bible Society for nearly fifty years, which is known for completing the first Hebrew version of the Old Testament, the *Tanakh*.

His most notable works include: *"A Critical Lexicon and Concordance to the English and Greek New Testament"* (1877); ***"Figures of Speech Used in the Bible"*** (1898); and notes and appendices to *"The Companion Bible"* (1909-1922 published posthumously).

He had a number of controversial theories on doctrines in the Bible. Shortly before his death, he changed his position on some. Regardless of his personal convictions, he left a legacy of works that students of the Bible still use today.

The following are examples of Bullinger's insight:

"All scripture was written for us, and for our learning; but they are not all addressed to us, or written concerning us."

"Christianity is religion; but religion in not necessarily Christianity. To say that a person is religious tells us nothing: for he may be a (insert any "religious" group) of any other religious system; but it does not follow that such a one is "in Christ and therefore a Christian."

God so loved the world, that he gave his
Only begotten
Son, that whosoever believes in him should not
Perish, but have
Everlasting
Life.   John 3:16

*The original 1898 version is updated as follows: Antiquated words and spellings appear in contemporary English. The text is large print in a visually consistent format. Webster's 1828 definitions are inserted in brackets [] to improve clarity and increase understanding. The 1611 King James Version (KJV) is converted to King James Today (KJT). Excerpts edited and expounded.

Figures of Speech Used in the Bible*
Explained and Illustrated
Ethelbert William (E.W.) Bullinger (1898)

INTRODUCTION

a) JEHOVAH has been pleased to give us the revelation of His mind and will in words. It is therefore absolutely necessary that we should understand not merely the meanings of the words themselves, but also the laws which govern their usage and combinations.

All language is governed by law; but, in order to increase the power of a word, or the force of an expression, these laws are **designedly departed** from, and words and sentences are thrown into, and used in, new forms, or *figures*.

The ancient Greeks reduced these new and peculiar forms to **science**, and gave names to more than two hundred of them.

The Romans carried forward this science: but with the decline of learning in the Middle Ages, it practically died out. A few writers have since then occasionally touched upon it briefly, and have given a few trivial examples: but the knowledge of this ancient science is so completely forgotten, that its very name today is used in a different sense and with almost an opposite meaning.

These manifold forms which words and sentences assume were called by the Greeks, Schema and by the Romans, Figura . Both words have the same meaning, viz., a shape or *figure*. When we speak of a person as being "a figure" we mean one who is dressed in some **peculiar style**, and **out of the ordinary manner**. The Greek word Schema is found in 1 Corinthians 7:31 , "The *fashion* of this world passes away"; Phillipians 2:8, "being found in *fashion* as a man." The Latin word Figura is from the verb fingere, to form, and has passed into the English language in the words *figure*, transfigure, configuration, effigy, feint, feign, etc., etc.

We use the word *figure* now in various senses. Its primitive meaning applies to any marks, lines, or outlines, which make a form or shape. Arithmetical figures are certain marks or forms which represent numbers (1, 2, 3, etc.). All secondary and derived meanings of the word "figure" retain this primitive meaning.

Applied to words, a *figure* denotes some form which a word or sentence takes, different from its ordinary and natural form. This is always for the purpose of giving additional force, more life, intensified feeling, and greater emphasis. Whereas today "*Figurative language*" is ignorantly spoken of as though it made less of the meaning, and deprived the words of their power and force. A passage of God's word is quoted; and it is met with the cry,"Oh, that is figurative"—implying that its meaning is weakened, or that it has quite a different meaning, or that it has no meaning at all. But the very opposite is the case. For an unusual form (figura) is never used except to add force to the truth conveyed, emphasis to the statement of it, and depth to the meaning of it. When we apply this science then to God's words and to Divine truths, we see at once that no branch of Bible study can be more important, or offer greater promise of substantial reward.

It lies at the very root of all translation; and it is the key to true interpretation... As the course of language moves smoothly along, according to the laws which govern it, there is nothing by which it can awaken or attract our attention. It is as when we are traveling by railway. As long as everything proceeds according to the regulations we notice nothing; we sleep, or we read, or meditate as the case may be. But, let the train slacken its speed, or make an unexpected stop;—we immediately hear the question asked, "What is the matter?" "What are we stopping for?" We hear one window go down and then another: attention is thoroughly aroused, and interest excited. So it is exactly with our reading. As long as all proceeds smoothly and according to law we notice nothing. But suddenly there is a departure from some law, a deviation from the even course—an unlooked for change—our attention is attracted, and we at once give our mind to discover why the words have been used in a new form, what the particular force of the passage is, and why we are to put special emphasis on the fact stated or on the truth conveyed. In fact, it is not too much to say that, in the use of these *figures*, we have, as it were, *the Holy Spirit's own markings of our Bibles*.

This is the most important point of all. For it is not by fleshly wisdom that the "words which the Holy Ghost teaches" are to be understood. **The natural man cannot understand the word of God. It is foolishness to him.** A man may admire a sun-dial, he may marvel at its use, and appreciate the cleverness of its design; he may be interested in its carved-work, or wonder at the mosaics or other beauties which adorn its structure: but, if he holds a lamp in his hand or any other light emanating from himself or from this world, he can make it any hour he pleases, and he will never be able to tell the time of day. Nothing but the light from God's sun in the Heavens can tell him that. So it is with the word of God. The natural man may admire its structure, or be interested in its statements; he may study its geography, its history, yea, even its prophecy; but **none of these things** will reveal to him his relation to time and eternity. Nothing but the light that comes from Heaven. **Nothing but the Sun of Righteousness can tell him that.** It may be said of the Bible, therefore, as it is of the New Jerusalem—"The Lamb is the light thereof." The Holy Spirit's work in this world is to lead to Christ, to glorify Christ. The Scriptures are inspired by the Holy Spirit; and the same Spirit that inspired the words in the Book must inspire its truths in our hearts, for they can and must be "Spiritually discerned" (1 Corinthians 2:1-16).

On this foundation, then, we have prosecuted this work.
And on these lines we have sought to carry it out.

We are dealing with the words "which the Holy Ghost teaches." All His works are perfect. *"The words of the Lord are pure words"*; human words, indeed, words pertaining to this world, but purified as silver is refined in a furnace. Therefore we must study every word, and in so doing we shall soon learn to say with Jeremiah (15:16), "Your WORDS were found, and I did eat them; and Your WORD was to me the joy and rejoicing of my heart."

It is clear, therefore, that no branch of Bible-study can be more important: and yet we may truly say that there is no branch of it which has been so utterly neglected.

c) A *figure* is, as we have before said, <u>a departure from the natural and</u>

fixed laws of Grammar or Syntax; but it is a departure not arising from ignorance or accident. Figures are not mere mistakes of Grammar; on the contrary, they are **legitimate** departures from law, for a special purpose. They are permitted variations with a particular object.

Therefore they are limited as to their number, and can be ascertained, named, and described.

No one is at liberty to exercise any arbitrary power in their use. All that art can do is to ascertain the laws to which nature has subjected them. There is no room for private opinion, neither can speculation concerning them have any authority.

It is not open to any one to say of this or that word or sentence, "This is a *figure*," according to his own fancy, or to suit his own purpose. We are dealing with a **science** whose laws and their workings are known. If a word or words be a *figure*, then that *figure* can be named, and described. It is used for a definite purpose and with a specific object. Man may use *figures* in ignorance, without any particular object. But when the Holy Spirit takes up human words and uses a *figure* (or peculiar form), it is for a special purpose, and that purpose must be observed and have due weight given to it.

Many misunderstood and perverted passages are difficult, only because we have not known the Lord's design in the difficulty.

Thomas Boys has well said (Commentary, 1 Peter 3), "There is much in the Holy Scriptures, which we find it hard to understand: nay, much that we seem to understand so fully as to imagine that we have discovered in it some difficulty or inconsistency. Yet the truth is, that passages of this kind are often the very parts of the Bible in which the greatest instruction is to be found: and, more than this, the instruction is to be obtained in the contemplation of the very difficulties by which at first we are startled. This is the intention of these apparent inconsistencies. The expressions are used, in order that we may mark them, dwell upon them, and draw instruction out of them. Things are put to us in a strange way, because, if they were put in a more ordinary way, we would not notice them."

This is true, not only of mere difficulties as such, but especially of all *Figures*: i.e., of all new and unwanted forms of words and speech: and our design in this work is that we should learn to notice them and gain the instruction they were intended to give us.

The word of God may, in one respect, be compared to the earth. All things necessary to life and sustenance may be obtained by scratching the surface of the earth: but there are treasures of beauty and wealth to be obtained by digging deeper into it. So it is with the Bible. "All things necessary to life and godliness" lie upon its surface for the humblest saint; but, beneath that surface are "great spoils" which are found only by those who seek after them as for "hid treasure."

THE PLAN OF THE WORK IS AS FOLLOWS:—

1. To give in its proper order and place each one of *two hundred and seventeen (217) figures of speech*, by name. **2.** Then to give the proper pronunciation of its name. **3.** Then its etymology, showing why the name was given to it, and what is its meaning. **4.** And, after this, a number of passages of Scripture, in full, where the figure is used, ranging from two or three instances, to some hundreds under each figure, accompanied by a full explanation. These special passages amount, in all, to nearly eight thousand (8,000).

We repeat, and it must be borne in mind, that all these many forms are employed only to set forth the truth with greater vigor and with a far greater meaning: and this, for the express purpose of indicating to us what is emphatic; and to call and attract our attention, so that it may be directed to, and fixed upon, the special truth which is to be conveyed to us.

Not every Figure is of equal importance, nor is every passage of equal interest.

But we advise all students of this great subject to go patiently forward, assuring them that from time to time they will be amply rewarded; and often when least expected.

NOTE: Bullinger's book contains 1105 pages. The ones that describe Figures of Speech in Psalm 1 will be included within this workbook.

Page 349 Second Division—**Figures involving Addition** [any thing added]

Figures involving addition are figures of speech which depend, for its new form, on some addition, either of **words** or of **sense**. In the one case, only the *words* are affected, by their repetition in various forms and ways. In the other, the addition is made to the *sense* by the use of other words.

All these various forms of repetition and addition are used for the purpose of attracting our attention, and of emphasizing what is said, which might otherwise be passed by unnoticed.

Figures involving **repetition** and **addition**

    I. Affecting words

        5. **Repetition of subjects**

Parallelism The repetition of similar, synonymous, or opposite subjects, thoughts, or words in parallel *[any thing equal to, like, or resembling another in all essential particulars or points]* or successive *[following in order or uninterrupted course, as a series of persons or things]* lines. Parallelism is universally treated as poetry. It is a form of the figure *Synonymia*, by which the subject of one line is repeated in the next line in different, but so-called, synonymous terms. There are seven kinds of parallelism, Psalm 1:1 uses **simple synonymous** or **gradational** parallelism.

Simple—**Synonymous or Gradational** *[a series of ascending steps or degrees, or a proceeding step by step; hence, progress from one degree or state to another; a regular advance from step to step]*. This is when the lines are parallel in thought, and in the use of synonymous *[conveying or expressing the same idea or thing]* words.

Note: In Parallelism "a line or lines" refer to **items in a list** *[a row or line, catalogue]*, **paired items** *[joined in couples]*, **a series** *[sequence; order; succession of things]*, and the like.

1 Below is a ❑ list, ❑ pair, ❑ series:

"Blessed is the man that walks not in the counsel of the ungodly,
            nor stands in the way of sinners,
            nor sits in the seat of the scornful." Psalm 1:1

Figures of Speech Used in the Bible *Today*—with Exercises

Back it up

2 Record the 3 verbs (*parts of grammar*) that state the action of the man:

1_____ 2_____ 3_____

3 Record the 3 nouns (person, place, thing (animal, object, idea):

1_____ 2_____ 3_____

4 Record the 2 adjectives that describe the noun and answers the "what kind of (fill in the blank with the noun being modified), or the verb":

1_____ 2_____ 3_____

Turn to page 89 to check your answers to the *parts of grammar* (adjective, noun, verb) noted after each phrase or word in the Psalm.

The following definitions should be understood to continue:

> **Similar** *[like; resembling; having a like form or appearance; it may signify exactly alike, or having a general likeness, a likeness in the principal points, or a likeness that is not perfect.]*
>
> **Synonymous** *[expressing the same thing; conveying the same idea.]*
>
> **Opposite** *[adverse; contrary; opposed.]*

5 Mark all that apply to Psalm 1:1:

❏ One line is repeated in the next line in different or similar terms.

❏ The repetition adds words. Only the words are affected by their repetition in various forms and ways.

❏ The repetition adds "the sense" *[perception by the intellect; discernment]*. Addition is made to "the sense" by the use of other words.

The use of poetic parallelism ❏ attracts attention ❏ emphasizes what is said ❏ made me notice what might have been unnoticed.

6 State why Psalm 1:1 is not **tautology** *[the needless repetition of a thing in different words or phrases]*.

_____

_____

_____

Figures of Speech Used in the Bible *Today*—with Exercises

RenewingLives.com

Back it up

7 Describe how walks/stands/sits is ❑ similar, ❑ synonymous, or ❑ opposite in ❑ thought and/or ❑ word?

_____

_____

8 Describe how counsel/way/seat is ❑ similar, ❑ synonymous, or ❑ opposite in ❑ thought and/or ❑ word?

_____

_____

9 Describe how ungodly,/sinners/scornful is ❑ similar, ❑ synonymous, or ❑ opposite in ❑ thought and/or ❑ word?

_____

_____

10 Describe how parallelism in Psalm 1:1 shows the **gradation** *[advancement, steps, or progress]* of the ungodly, plus any wisdom you have gained.

_____

_____

_____

_____

_____

_____

_____

_____

_____

_____

_____

Back it up

Page 429 Second Division—**Figures involving Addition** [any thing added]

Figures involving addition are figures of speech which depend, for its new form, on some addition, either of **words** or of **sense**. In the one case, only the *words* are affected, by their repetition in various forms and ways. In the other, the addition is made to the *sense* by the use of other words.

Figures involving repetition and addition

II. Affecting the sense (figures of rhetoric)

We now pass from figures more closely affecting Grammar *[a system of general principles and of particular rules for speaking or writing a language]* and Syntax *[the construction of sentences; the due arrangement of words in sentences, according to established usage]* to those which relate to **Rhetoric** *[the art of speaking with propriety, elegance and force; the power of persuasion or attraction; that which allures or charms]*. Figures, which not merely affect the *meaning* of words, but the *use and application* of words. These figures of repetition and addition of sense rather than of words are *used in reasoning*. Sometimes the same sense is repeated in other words. Sometimes the words themselves are repeated, but always by way of *amplifying the sense* for purposes of *definition, emphasis, or explanation*.

II. Affecting the sense, by way of

2. Amplification

Gradual Ascent/Anabasis An increase of sense in successive *[following in order or uninterrupted course, as a series of persons or things]* sentences.

The figure is so called when a writing, speech, or discourse *[communication of thoughts by words, either to individuals, companies, or public assemblies]* ascends *[moves upwards; rises]* up step-by-step, each with an increase of emphasis or sense. When this increase or ascent is from weaker to stronger expression, and is confined to words, it is called *Climax*. When the sense or gradation is downward instead of upward, it is called *Catabasis*. This increase is often connected with Parallelism. When the increase is not a mere increase of vehemence *[violence; great force]*, or of evil, but leads up from things inferior to things superior; from things terrestial *[things of, on, or relating to the earth]* to things celestial *[belonging or relating to heaven]*; from things mundane *[belonging to the world]* to things spiritual; the figure is called *Anagoge*.

"Blessed is the man that walks not in the counsel of the ungodly,
          nor stands in the way of sinners,
          nor sits in the seat of the scornful." Psalm 1:1

1 What is rhetoric?

_____

_____

2 E.W. Bullinger's Psalm 1:1 comments: Here is a triple *Anabasis* depending on Parallelism:

- The first are impious *[irreverent towards the Supreme Being]*, as to their mind.

- The second are sinners, who not only think, but carry out the workings of their evil *[bad, corrupt, injurious, perverse, wicked]* minds.

- The third are scorners *[a despiser who mocks at sin]*, glorying in their wickedness *[evil practices]* and scoffing *[ridicules, mocks]* at righteousness *[one that is observant of the divine commands in practice with affection for holiness]*.

Again,

- The first continue in that mind, taking evil counsel.

- The second carry it out, as the principle of their walk.

- The third settle down in their evil, as on a seat.

How do Bullinger's comments improve your understanding of Psalm 1:1?

_____

_____

_____

_____

_____

_____

_____

Figures of Speech Used in the Bible *Today*—with Exercises

Page 727 Third Division—**Figures involving Change** *[to cause to turn or pass from one state to another; to alter or make different; to vary in external form or in essence.]*

Figures involving change are figures of speech where the figure consists of a change affecting the meaning, use, arrangement, and order of words, phrases, and sentences: also changes affecting the application of words. Under this division come all the figures of change as to both *syntax [the construction of sentences; the due arrangement of words in sentences, according to established usage]* and *rhetoric [the art of speaking with propriety, elegance and force; the power of persuasion or attraction; that which allures or charms]*.

Figures involving **change**

III. Affecting the **application** of words.

We now come to the last class of the three great divisions of figurative language, figures which involve the ***application*** of words rather than their **meaning** or **order** .

These we propose to consider under those that have to do with change; not that there is any real or absolute change; but because there is a deviation or change from the literal *[real; exact]*, or from the more ordinary and usual application of words. This change is brought about and prompted by some internal action of the mind, which seeks to impress its intensity of feeling upon others. The meaning of the words themselves continues to be literal: the figure lies in the application of the words. This application arises from some actual resemblance between the words, or between two or more mental things which are before the mind.

When the literal application of the words is contrary to ordinary plain human experience, or to the nature of the things themselves, then we are compelled to regard the application as figurative, though the words themselves still retain their literal meaning; otherwise, the application would lose all its force and all its point.

Figures involving change

III. Affecting the **application** of words.

1. As to **sense**

Resemblance/Simile A declaration that one thing resembles another; or, comparison by resemblance. This figure has no corresponding Greek name. Indeed it can hardly be called a figure, or an unusual form of expression, seeing it is quite literal, and one of the commonest forms of expression in use. It is a cold, clear, plain statement as to a resemblance between words and things. The whole application of the figure lies in this resemblance , and not in representation, as in *metonymy*; or in implication, as in *hypocatastasis*; or, in association, as in *synecdoche*.

Accordingly, when this resemblance is not apparent, or is counter to our ordinary perception of things, it jars upon the ear. Such similes abound in human writings. Hence the pleasure of studying the use of them in the word of God, where we have the Holy Spirit's own perfect work.

Many examples could be given of false, or incongruous similes in human writings. No such inexplicable similes as these can be found in the Scriptures. When one is used there, it is "for our learning;" and the more we study it the more we may learn.

They are usually marked by "like as" or, by other kindred words "as", "even as", "inasmuch as", "just as", "like", etc.

Simile differs from *comparison*, in that comparison admits of dissimilitudes as well as resemblances.

Simile differs from *allegory* in that allegory names only one of the two things and leaves us to find, and make the resemblance with the other, ourselves.

Simile differs from *metaphor* in that it merely states resemblance, while metaphor boldly transfers the representation.

Simile differs from *hypocatastasis* in that the latter only implies the resemblance, while simile states it.

Simile , therefore, is destitute of feeling. It is clear, beautiful, gentle, true to fact, but cold and too deliberate for passion.

All this will be seen as the similes are studied. They require no explanation. They explain and are intended to explain themselves. It is scarcely necessary to give any examples. They abound throughout the Scripture *[the Bible]*, and impart *[to give, grant or communicate]* to it much of its beauty and force.

1 What is rhetoric?

_____

_____

2 A simile involves a ❑ change ❑ deviation affecting the ❑ application ❑ meaning or ❑ order of words, phrases, and sentences.

3 In a simile, the ❑ literal *[real; exact]*, ❑ ordinary, ❑ usual application of words prompts the mind with an impression of feeling.

4 In a simile, ❑ the literal *[real; exact]* meaning ❑ the application of words changes.

5 A simile creates a resemblance between ❑ words ❑ mental things before the mind.

6 A simile creates a "mental picture". ❑ Y ❑ N ❑?

7 A simile is used to add force to a point being made. ❑ Y ❑ N ❑?

8 A simile is a ❑ cold ❑ clear ❑ plain statement as to a resemblance between ❑ words ❑ things.

9 A simile is a declaration that one thing ❑ resembles, ❑ represents, ❑ implies ❑ associates with another.

10 A simile causes you to pay attention to a resemblance that ❑ is not apparent, ❑ is counter to our ordinary perception of things.

11 Kindred words to simile can be: ❑ as, ❑ even as, ❑ inasmuch as, ❑ just as, ❑ like, ❑ like as.

12 How does a simile differ from a comparison?

_____

_____

_____

Figures of Speech Used in the Bible *Today*—with Exercises

13 How does a simile differ from an allegory?

_____

_____

_____

14 How does a simile differ from a metaphor?

_____

_____

_____

15 How does a simile differ from an hypocatastasis/implication?

_____

_____

_____

16 A simile is used to add ❑ beauty ❑ force in the Scriptures.

Bullinger's Comments:

Psalm 1:3a **"He shall be like a tree planted by the rivers of water..."** Here, the similitude *[likeness; resemblance; likeness in nature, qualities of appearance]* tells us that the man who meditates in God's word is planted and protected, just as a tree in a garden is cared for as a "tree of the field" is not.

Psalm 1:4 **"The ungodly are not so: but are like the chaff which the wind drives away."**

The contrast *[to set in opposition two or more figures of a like kind, with a view to show the difference or dissimilitude, and to manifest the superior excellence of the one by the inferiority of the other, or to exhibit the excellence of the one and the defects of the other in a more striking view]* between the driven chaff and the "planted" tree is most striking and solemn *[adapted to impress seriousness, gravity or reverence]*.

Figures of Speech Used in the Bible *Today*—with Exercises

Back it up

Bullet Points *[used to signify importance; any point worthy of special emphasis.]*

- _____
- _____
- _____
- _____
- _____
- _____
- _____
- _____
- _____
- _____
- _____
- _____

Back it up

RenewingLives.com

Back it up—Insight, lists, questions, notes, thoughts, etc.

Express it

"You can't understand the word of God
unless you understand the words."™

❏ **Express it**—The fifth and final step encourages you to express your learning and yourself in various creative ways. This is the part where you apply what you've read, observed, and confirmed as true in the previous steps. ***This means you should complete the previous steps before enjoying this final step,*** *which can be considered "the fun stuff."*

Expression of self can be shown in many ways, including: *asking questions, call to action, communicating your beliefs, creative writing, evaluating relationships, graphic arts, journaling, memorization, paraphrasing scripture, personalizing God's word, responding to or creating questions, responding to God's word, self-test.*

You may find some activities help reduce stress, while others challenge your brain. Some are fun, some are serious.

The following pages are in alphabetical order (based on the title given) but can be completed in any order. Enjoy!

Express it

Acts—verb transitive *[deed, do, perform, work]* & **Actions**—noun *[acting or moving]*

1 Is there an error I can **correct** [*Literally, set right, or made straight, hence, right; conformable to truth, rectitude or propriety, or conformable to a just standard; not faulty; free from error; to make right; to rectify; to bring to the standard of truth, justice, or propriety; to amend; to remove or retrench faults or errors; to set right; to bring back or attempt to bring back to propriety in morals; to obviate or remove whatever is wrong or inconvenient; to reduce or change the qualities of any thing by mixture, or other application; to counteract whatever is injurious.]*?

_____

_____

_____

2 Is there any good I could do in **deed** *[that which is done, acted or effected; an act; a fact; a word of extensive application, including whatever is done, good or bad, great or small; exploit (a deed or act, more especially, a heroic act; a deed of renown; a great or noble achievement); illustrious (conspicuous; distinguished by the reputation of greatness; renowned; eminent; glorious); act; power of action or agency.]*?

_____

_____

_____

3 Of my family, friends, or enemies is there something I should give in kindness as a **gift** *[a present; any thing, the property of which is voluntarily transferred by one person to another without compensation; a donation; the act, right or power of bestowing, conferring, or giving; an offering or oblation (any thing offered or presented in worship or sacred service; an offering; a sacrifice); a reward.]*?

_____

_____

_____

Express it

Acts & Actions *(continued)*

4 Of someone I choose, what action could I take to build a better **relationship** *[the state of being related by kindred (relative by birth, blood, or marriage; connection in kind), affinity (the relation contracted by marriage, between a husband and his wife's kindred, and between a wife and her husband's kindred); or other alliance; a person connected by consanguinity (the relation or connection of persons descended from the same stock or common ancestor); connection between things]?*

_____

_____

_____

_____

5 Of anything that comes to mind, how could I have handled it **better** *[having good qualities in a greater degree than another; more advantageous, acceptable, safe; have the advantage, improvement, superiority, or victory; more correctly, or fully; with superior excellence; with more affection; in a higher degree; to advance, or exceed; to support or give advantage to.]?*

_____

_____

_____

_____

6 Of anything that comes to mind, what will I do **differently** *[in a different manner; distinct; separate; not the same]?*

_____

_____

_____

_____

_____

Express it

RenewingLives.com

Application—noun *[in sermons of religious instruction grounded on some text or passage of Scripture, that part of the discourse, in which the principles before laid down and illustrated, are applied to practical uses; the act of putting something to use.]*

Make a practical conclusion. Share the lesson you derived from spending time in God's word. How can you *personally apply* what you learned?

_____

_____

_____

_____

_____

_____

_____

_____

_____

_____

_____

_____

_____

_____

_____

_____

_____

_____

_____

_____

Express it

Bible Verse Art Instructions

One creative way to meditate on God's word is to choose a verse or portion of one to create visual art. You can create a poster, bookmarker, or draw directly in the margin of your Bible. Some people refer to this as "Bible Journaling," but traditionally, journaling is the expression of thoughts on paper. To keep written journaling separate from art journaling, the phrase Bible Verse Art is used.

Supplies used for Bible Verse Art might include a pencil, eraser, pens, highlighters, watercolor pencils or paint, stamps, washi tape *[decorative thin masking tape]*, or stickers. Following are helpful tips:

☞Choose a verse or portion of one, then read it a few times. Think of what the verse means to you and how you might express the words in an art form. Studying the verse will help your creativity flow from having a better understanding of its meaning and message.

☞Determine which word or words communicate the main message, the most important part of the verse, or ones that stand out to you for any reason.

☞Use a pencil to sketch your design, leaving room for the remainder of the text and drawing. Use your eraser to adjust your art until you are happy with the results, then finalize it with darker lines or by adding color.

☞Add symbols, icons, logos, doodles, or any graphic you are inspired to trace or create. You don't need to be "artistic" to enjoy the freedom of being creative.

☞You might want to sign and date your art, then consider blessing someone with your creation.

Express it

RenewingLives.com

Bible Verse Art

1) Pick a verse from the chapter. **2)** Sketch in the words you want to bring attention to first—leaving space to add the rest of the verse above, below, or around it. **3)** Use your imagination to make the verse visually expressive.

Express it

Bible Word Art

Draw one word or phrase from the chapter, making it visually expressive.

Express it

RenewingLives.com

Bumper/Window Sticker Art

Inspired by something *from the chapter*, create bumper or window sticker designs that are wholesome *[contributing to the health of the mind; favorable to morals, religion or prosperity; conducive to public happiness, virtue, or peace]*.

Post-in' Notes & Quotes

Express it

Renewinglives.com

Called by His Grace

Called—participle passive *[invited; called to some office; divinely selected and appointed.]*

"But when it pleased God, who separated me from my mother's womb, and called me by his grace, to reveal his Son in me, that I might preach him among the heathen... Galatians 1:15-16a *(the words of Paul, the apostle)*

Grace—noun *[the divine influence upon the heart and its reflection in the life; including gratitude; properly, that which affords joy, pleasure, delight, sweetness, charm, loveliness: good-will, loving-kindness, favor; kindness which bestows upon one what he has not deserved; that kindness by which God bestows favors even upon the ill-deserving, and grants to sinners the pardon of their offenses and bids them accept of eternal salvation; through pity for sinful men Christ left his state of blessedness with God in heaven and voluntarily underwent the hardships and miseries of human life, and by his sufferings and death procured salvation for mankind; the merciful kindness by which God, exerting his holy influence upon souls, turns them to Christ, keeps, strengthens, increases them in Christian faith, knowledge, affection, and kindles them to the exercise of the Christian virtues; the favor of Christ, assisting and strengthening his followers and ministers to bear their troubles.]*

All true Believers are saints *[set apart for God to lead a life acceptable to Him]* and called *[appointed, invited, selected]* to do God's purposes. Some answer the call to preach, proclaiming the gospel *[good news]*. Others are prophets, teachers, or used in the distribution of miracles and healing. Some give of their time and talents through helps, administration (such as governing and directing church affairs), sharing God's truth in another tongue, or interpreting. There are many different ways to serve the Lord. These are just a few.

1 What spiritually-minded things are you drawn to or interested in:

_____

_____

_____

2 If you knew it wouldn't pay a penny, name something you'd enjoy doing:

_____

_____

_____

Express it

Called by His Grace *(continued)*

3 What do others notice you are good or gifted at?

_____

_____

_____

4 What do you think your "calling" might be?

_____

_____

_____

5 If you knew you couldn't fail, what would you do to serve the Lord and others?

_____

_____

_____

6 Name one thing you enjoyed doing (for another's benefit) in the past week:

_____

_____

_____

7 In what way do you minister *[attend and serve; give things needful; supply the means of relief; to relieve]* to someone?

_____

_____

_____

8 How does grace tie in with being called?

_____

_____

_____

_____

RenewingLives.com

Express it

Creative Writing: Composition—noun *[in literature, the act of inventing or combining ideas, clothing them with words, arranging them in order, and in general, committing them to paper, i.e., writing an original work.]*

Express it

Creative Writing: Poem —noun *[a composition in which the verses (a line of writing containing a certain number of long and short syllable words) consist of certain measures, whether in blank verse (non-rhyming) or in rhyme (repetition of words with similar or nearly the same sounds.)]*

_____

_____

_____

_____

_____

_____

_____

_____

_____

_____

_____

_____

_____

_____

_____

_____

_____

_____

_____

_____

Express it

RenewingLives.com

Creative Writing: Song —noun *[in general, that which is sung or uttered with musical modulations of the voice, whether of the human voice or that of a bird; a little poem to be sung; a ballad; a sacred poem or hymn to be sung either in joy or thanksgiving.]*

_____

_____

_____

_____

_____

_____

_____

_____

_____

_____

_____

_____

_____

_____

_____

_____

_____

_____

_____

_____

_____

Express it

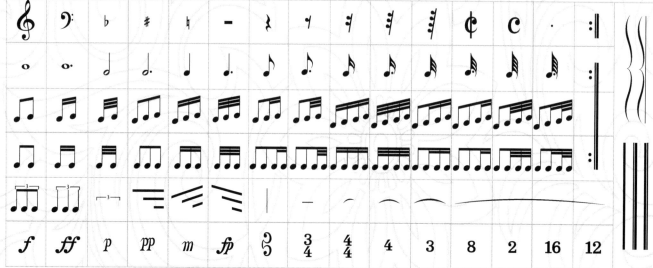

Express it

Renewing Lives.com

Friend or Foe

Advocate—noun *[an intercessor, consoler, comforter; summoned, called to one's side to aid; one who pleads another's cause before a judge; counsel for defense; a helper, succorer, assistant; one who defends, vindicates, or espouses a cause, by argument; one who is friendly to.]*

"My little children, these things write I to you, that you sin not. And if any man sin, we have an advocate with the Father, Jesus Christ the righteous:" 1 John 2:1

Friend—noun *[an associate (more or less close); a brother; companion; fellow; friend, husband, lover, neighbor; one who is attached to another by affection; one who entertains for another's sentiments of esteem, respect and affection, which lead him to desire his company, and to seek to promote his happiness and prosperity.]*

"A man that has friends must show himself friendly: and there is a friend that sticks closer than a brother." Proverbs 18:24

or

Adversary—noun *[an enemy or foe; one who has enmity at heart; an opponent or antagonist=one who contends with another in combat; to press, compress; bind up; oppress.]*

"Be sober, be vigilant; because your adversary the devil, as a roaring lion, walks about, seeking whom he may devour:" 1 Peter 5:8

Enemy—noun *[a foe; an adversary; a private enemy is one who hates another and wishes him injury, or attempts to do him injury to gratify his own malice or ill will; one who hates or dislikes; in theology, and by way of eminence, the enemy is the Devil; the archfiend.]*

"And he saved them from the hand of him that hated them, and redeemed them from the hand of the enemy." Psalm 106:10

Foe—noun *[an enemy; one who entertains personal enmity=ill will; hatred; malevolence=evil disposition towards another; inclination to injure others), grudge, hatred, or malice against another; an enemy in war; one of a nation at war with another, whether he entertains enmity against the opposing nation or not; an adversary; an opposing army, or nation at war; An opponent; an enemy; one who opposes any thing in principle; an ill-wisher.]*

"...behold, there stood a man over against him with his sword drawn in his hand: and Joshua went unto him, and said to him, Are you for us (friend)**, or for our adversaries** (foe)**?"** Joshua 5:13b   *(words in parenthesis added for clarity)*

Express it

Friend or Foe *(continued)*

Psalm 1 should cause you to consider who you spend time with. Determine who might have an influence on you, then choose a category based on the definitions provided. Note any good/bad qualities you should consider.

Ac =Advocate, Fr=Friend **or** *As=Adversary, E=Enemy, Fo=Foe*

Person _____ ❏ Ac ❏ Fr *or* ❏ As ❏ E ❏ Fo

_____

_____

Person _____ ❏ Ac ❏ Fr *or* ❏ As ❏ E ❏ Fo

_____

_____

Person _____ ❏ Ac ❏ Fr *or* ❏ As ❏ E ❏ Fo

_____

_____

Person _____ ❏ Ac ❏ Fr *or* ❏ As ❏ E ❏ Fo

_____

_____

Person _____ ❏ Ac ❏ Fr *or* ❏ As ❏ E ❏ Fo

_____

_____

Person _____ ❏ Ac ❏ Fr *or* ❏ As ❏ E ❏ Fo

_____

_____

Person _____ ❏ Ac ❏ Fr *or* ❏ As ❏ E ❏ Fo

_____

_____

Goal Preparation—noun *[to take the necessary previous measures, make ready.]*

The focus of my goal is: ❑ adventure ❑ to break a bad habit
❑ creative ❑ educational ❑ family ❑ financial ❑ fitness
❑ job/career/vocation/business ❑ social ❑ spiritual ❑ start good habit
❑ time management ❑ travel ❑ volunteering ❑ another goal.

It is a ❑ first-step ❑ short-term ❑ long-term ❑ lifetime goal.

1 What specific thing(s) do you want to **achieve** *[to perform; to accomplish; to finish or carry on to a final close; to gain or obtain, as the result of exertion]*?

_____

_____

2 How does your goal differ from a **dream** *[to have ideas or images in the mind; to waste time in vain thoughts; daydream; fantasy (imagine impossible or improbable things)]*?

_____

_____

3 What do you **hope** *[a desire of some good, accompanied with at least a slight expectation of obtaining it, or a belief that it is obtainable]*?

_____

_____

4 How does your goal differ from **luck** *[receiving some unforeseen, unexpected good, or good which was not dependent on one's own effort, power, or skill]*?

_____

_____

5 What action are you taking to create a **plan** *[a scheme devised; the form of something to be done existing in the mind, an idea, expressed in words or committed to writing]*?

_____

_____

6 In what way(s) is your goal **realistic** *[based on what is real rather than on what is wanted or hoped for; obtainable given the talent and resources you really have]*?

_____

_____

7 In what way(s) does your goal differ from a **wish** *[to have a desire or longing for what is or is not supposed to be obtainable; something that cannot or probably will not happen]*?

_____

Express it

My Goal—noun *[the end or final purpose you aim to reach or accomplish by successful exertions.]*

Record your goal on line #1. Ask yourself **what needs to be done to** reach #1, then to reach #2. Continue all the way up to #20 which should be a small or easy action you begin with, and once completed, it builds confidence.

Action/Plan/Task   Month/Year

20 ❏ _____ _____ ❏

19 ❏ _____ _____ ❏

18 ❏ _____ _____ ❏

17 ❏ _____ _____ ❏

16 ❏ _____ _____ ❏

15 ❏ _____ _____ ❏

14 ❏ _____ _____ ❏

13 ❏ _____ _____ ❏

12 ❏ _____ _____ ❏

11 ❏ _____ _____ ❏

10 ❏ _____ _____ ❏

9 ❏ _____ _____ ❏

8 ❏ _____ _____ ❏

7 ❏ _____ _____ ❏

6 ❏ _____ _____ ❏

5 ❏ _____ _____ ❏

4 ❏ _____ _____ ❏

3 ❏ _____ _____ ❏

2 ❏ _____ _____ ❏

#1 _____ _____ ❏

Express it

Godly/Good versus *[in contrast to]* Ungodly/Evil in the Bible

Godly—adjective *[kind; holy, merciful; gracious; God-like; pious; reverencing God, his character, and laws; living in obedience to God's commands from a principle of love to him and reverence of his character and precepts; religious; righteous; conformed to God's law.]*

"But know that the LORD has set apart him that is godly for himself: the LORD will hear when I call to him." Psalm 4:3

Good—adjective, adverb *[valid; sound; not weak, false; fallacious; complete or sufficiently perfect in its kind; having the physical qualities best adapted to its design and use; having moral qualities best adapted to its design and use, or the qualities which God's law requires; virtuous; pious; religious; applied to persons, and opposed to bad, vicious, wicked, evil; conformable to the moral law; conducive to happiness; useful; valuable; having qualities or a tendency to produce a good effect; kind; benevolent; affectionate; faithful; promotive of happiness; well; beautiful; best; better; bountiful; cheerful; at ease; be in favor; glad; graciously; joyful; loving; most pleasant; pleases; pleasure; precious; prosperity; ready; sweet; wealth; welfare; well-favored.]*

"For you, Lord, are good, and ready to forgive; and plenteous in mercy to all them that call upon you." Psalm 86:5

or

Ungodly—adjective *[morally wrong; an (actively) bad person, condemned, guilty and liable to punishment; unrighteous; impious; neglecting the fear and worship of God, or violating his commands; sinful; contrary to the divine commands; polluted by wickedness.]*

"For the LORD knows the way of the righteous: but the way of the ungodly shall perish." Psalm 1:6

Evil—adjective *[to be unjust or injurious; to defraud; having bad qualities of a natural or moral kind; mischievous; having qualities which tend to injury, or to produce mischief; wicked; corrupt; perverse; wrong; unfortunate; unhappy; producing sorrow, distress, injury or calamity; natural evil is any thing which produces pain, distress, loss or calamity, or which in any way disturbs the peace, impairs the happiness, or destroys the perfection of natural beings; moral evil is any deviation of a moral agent from the rules of conduct prescribed to him by God, or by legitimate human authority, or it is any violation of the plain principles of justice and rectitude; adversity; affliction; calamity; displeasure; distress; grievous; harm; hurtful; ill-favored; misery; naughty; sad; sorrow; trouble; vex; wicked one; worse; wretchedness; wrong.]*

"The face of the LORD is against them that do evil, to cut off the remembrance of them from the earth." Psalm 34:6

Express it

Godly/Good versus Ungodly/Evil *(continued)*

Psalm 1 should cause you to consider the behavior of others as well as your own. List each person you listen to, take advice from, or would ask for help.

Gl=Godly, Gd=Good or U=Ungodly, E=Evil

Person _____ ❑ Gl ❑ Gd *or* ❑ U ❑ E

_____

_____

Person _____ ❑ Gl ❑ Gd *or* ❑ U ❑ E

_____

_____

Person _____ ❑ Gl ❑ Gd *or* ❑ U ❑ E

_____

_____

Person _____ ❑ Gl ❑ Gd *or* ❑ U ❑ E

_____

_____

Person _____ ❑ Gl ❑ Gd *or* ❑ U ❑ E

_____

_____

Person _____ ❑ Gl ❑ Gd *or* ❑ U ❑ E

_____

_____

Me _____ ❑ Gl ❑ Gd *or* ❑ U ❑ E

_____

_____

_____

Express it

Grace & Mercy

Grace—noun *[kindness; favor; beauty; good-will; kindness which bestows upon one what he has not deserved; the free unmerited love and favor of God, the spring and source of all the benefits men receive from Him; the manner or act of divine influence upon the heart and its reflection in life including gratitude; that which affords joy, pleasure, delight, sweetness, charm, loveliness; loving-kindness; favorable influence of God; divine influence or the influence of the Spirit, in renewing the heart and restraining from sin; the application of Christs' righteousness to the sinner.]*

"Surely he scorns the scorners: but he gives grace to the lowly." Proverbs 3:34

Mercy—noun *[pity to one in misfortune; by implication towards God, piety; kindness; favor; beauty; goodness; to be compassionate by word or deed, especially by divine grace; to have compassion or pity on; to succor one afflicted or seeking aid; to bring help to the wretched; specifically of God granting even to the unworthy favor, benefits, opportunities, and particularly salvation by Christ; that benevolence, mildness or tenderness of heart which disposes a person to overlook injuries, or to treat an offender better than he deserves; the disposition that tempers justice, and induces an injured person to forgive trespasses and injuries, and to forbear punishment, or inflict less than law or justice will warrant. In this sense, there is perhaps no word in our language precisely synonymous with mercy. That which comes nearest to it is grace. Mercy implies benevolence, tenderness, mildness, pity or compassion, and clemency, but exercised only towards offenders; mercy is a distinguishing attribute of the Supreme Being; pity; compassion manifested towards a person in distress; the act of sparing, or the forbearance of a violent act expected; to be or to lie at the mercy of, to have no means of self-defense, but to be dependent for safety on the mercy or compassion of another, or in the power of that which is irresistible.]*

"Remember not the sins of my youth, nor my transgressions: according to your mercy remember you me for your goodness' sake, O LORD." Psalm 25:7

Note: There is a distinction between grace and mercy, but they are closely related. Both include favor and kindness. Grace contains the idea of bestowing a gift of favor. Since grace begins with a G, remember, "***Grace* is a g*ift*."**

Mercy is granted to one in misery *[great unhappiness; extreme pain of body or mind]*. Out of mercy, an offender is treated better than he/she deserves. Since mercy begins with an M, remember, "***Mercy* is for the m*iserable*."**

Express it

Grace & Mercy *(continued)*

Psalm 1 should cause you to consider your need for grace and mercy. Write about circumstances in your life that would call for each. *G=Grace, M=Mercy*

❑ G ❑ M _____

_____

_____

_____

_____

_____

_____

_____

_____

❑ G ❑ M _____

_____

_____

_____

_____

_____

_____

_____

Express it

RenewingLives.com

I Believe—verb transitive *[to credit upon the authority or testimony of another; to be persuaded of the truth of something upon the declaration of another, or upon evidence furnished by reasons, arguments, and deductions of the mind, or by circumstances other than personal knowledge; to expect or hope with confidence; to trust; In theology, to believe sometimes expresses a mere assent of the understanding to the truths of the gospel; as in the case of Simon. Acts 8:37. In others, the word implies, with this assent of the mind, a yielding of the will and affections, accompanied with a humble reliance on Christ for salvation. John 1:12. John 3:15.]*

Answer the questions with **Y** for Yes, **N** for No, *and* ? *if you aren't sure.*

1 Good works help me earn entrance to heaven ....Y.... N ...?

2 Jesus Christ revealed in the New Testament
   is the anointed Messiah of the Old Testament ....Y.... N ...?

3 There is only one Lord God Almighty ....Y.... N ...?

4 Jesus died after being crucified (nailed to a cross, tortured) .....Y.... N ...?

5 Jesus Christ is God's only begotten (only-born; sole) Son.........Y.... N ...?

6 When I die, I will go directly to heaven ....Y.... N ...?

7 I cannot avoid death...Y.... N ...?

8 I fall short of perfection—I am a sinner................................Y.... N ...?

9 I need God's gracious free gift of salvation...........................Y.... N ...?

10 Jesus Christ is God in the flesh, come to Earth.......................Y.... N ...?

11 Unrepentant, unforgiven sin separates me from a right
   relationship with God and others.......................................Y.... N ...?

12 Because Jesus conquered death, I too can be raised
   to eternal life after death ....Y.... N ...?

13 Jesus died on the cross to pay the penalty for my sins,
   past, present, and future...Y.... N ...?

14 Nothing I can accomplish or work for deserves
   eternal life or heaven ....Y.... N ...?

15 Being a good person gets me into heaven ....Y.... N ...?

16 Something I've done is unforgivable ....Y.... N ...?

Xpress it

I Believe (continued)

17 I get to choose the consequences for my sin.................................Y.... N ...?

18 Hell is a real/actual/literal place of punishment ....Y.... N ...?

19 I am a servant of Christ ....Y.... N ...?

20 Jesus Christ is "Emmanuel" God with us ....Y.... N ...?

21 God is the perfect, holy, just, righteous, Creator........................Y.... N ...?

22 My life changed after receiving Christ as Lord and Savior ....Y.... N ...?

23 To receive Christ, I must first change my lifestyle....................Y.... N ...?

24 Repent means to "turn from my sin," like a U-turn....................Y.... N ...?

25 Repent means "have a change of mind," to choose differently ..Y.... N ...?

26 I am righteous because of my own efforts ....Y.... N ...?

27 I have been saved by faith in Jesus Christ alone ....Y.... N ...?

28 The Holy Spirit dwells/lives in believers in Christ.....................Y.... N ...?

29 God won't allow sin or evil to go unpunished............................Y.... N ...?

30 All sin is ultimately against God/Jesus Christ...........................Y.... N ...?

31 Eternal death is a just punishment for sin.................................Y.... N ...?

32 No one is good, except God/Jesus/Holy Spirit ....Y.... N ...?

33 The only way to get to heaven is through Jesus........................Y.... N ...?

34 Jesus Christ, God in the flesh, is the only one who
can forgive me of my sin. ....Y.... N ...?

35 Christ rules and reigns in my heart/mind...................................Y.... N ...?

36 I'm 100% confident I am not going to hell.................................Y.... N ...?

37 I trust in Jesus Christ as the One I go to for advice,
wisdom and direction..Y.... N ...?

38 Sin no longer "controls" or has power over me. ....Y.... N ...?

39 I've been "born again," according to John 3.............................Y.... N ...?

40 If you answered "No" to question 39, what would convince you Jesus
Christ is God's only Son and the only "door" to everlasting life:

Share your completed form with a Bible teacher, chaplain, minister, pastor, seasoned believer, etc., especially if you are unsure or have questions.

Express it

RenewingLives.com

Express it

Name: _____ Date __/__/____

My Journal —noun *[a record of experiences, ideas, or reflections meant for private use.]*

_____

_____

_____

_____

_____

_____

_____

_____

_____

_____

_____

_____

_____

_____

_____

_____

_____

_____

_____

_____

_____

_____

_____

_____

Express it

My Journal *(continued)*

My Testimony—noun *[a declaration or affirmation made to establish or prove fact; open attestation (witness; a solemn or official declaration, verbal or written, in support of a fact; evidence).]*   *Use additional paper if desired.*

1 Who I was before I received Jesus Christ as my Lord and Savior:

_____

_____

_____

2 What adjective *[used to inquire of the identity, nature or value of an object, person, or matter; specifies form or manner; a way of acting or being, class or order, rank, condition or quality; distinct particulars]* **caused me to have a want to have a change of heart, or disposition** *[temper]*, **in which the enmity** *[enemy, opposite of friendship, hatred]* **of my heart to God and his law and the obstinacy** *[stubborn, unyielding]* **of my will were subdued** *[brought to subjection, overpowered, tamed, conquered]*, **and succeeded by supreme love to God, His moral government, and a reformation** *[correcting what is wrong; amending; restoring to a good state; forming anew]* **of my life:**

_____

_____

_____

3 Where adverb *[at, in or to which place or situation]* **I was as I received Christ:**

_____

_____

4 When adverb *[indicates circumstance or time]* **I received Christ:**

_____

_____

5 Why adverb *[for what cause, purpose, or reason]* **I finally realized I needed God and the power of His Holy Spirit through Jesus Christ my Lord and Savior:**

_____

_____

_____

Express it

My Testimony *(continued)*

6 How adverb *[in what manner, means or way; to what degree or extent; or used to ask about the condition or quality of something]* **my life is different since receiving Christ:**

_____

_____

_____

_____

_____

_____

_____

_____

_____

_____

_____

_____

_____

_____

_____

_____

_____

_____

_____

Express it

RenewingLives.com

Pause to Ponder—verb transitive *[to weigh in the mind; to consider and compare the circumstances or consequences of an event, or the importance of the reasons for or against a decision; to view with deliberation; to examine.]*

Bk _____Chpt _____ Verse _____

1 As a **tutor** *[one who has the care of instructing another in any branch of human learning]* (❏ aunt/uncle, ❏ caregiver, ❏ friend, ❏ grandparent, ❏ guardian, ❏ parent, ❏ sibling, ❏ _____) of *this person* I love:_____ the *above verse* captured my attention *because*:

_____

_____

_____

2 The verse reveals the nature *[essential qualities of something; system of created things; peculiar qualities distinguished from others]* of ❏ God, ❏ His children, ❏ mankind, ❏ unbeliever's, and/or ❏ this world and its viewpoint *in this way*:

_____

_____

_____

3 The verse I chose speaks to my heart/mind regarding my ❏ behavior, ❏ focus, ❏ plan(s), or ❏ pursuit(s) *because:*

_____

_____

_____

4 ❏ My, ❏ my loved one's ❏ actions, ❏ attitude, and/or ❏ words need to adjust to line up with God's standards *in the following way(s):*

_____

_____

_____

5 Since my loved one is not always in my presence or under my supervision, I can use the teaching in the verse to guide her/him *in this way:*

_____

_____

_____

Express it

Pause to Ponder _(continued)_

6 From my perspective, the chapter/verse I chose _teaches this_ life lesson _[something that teaches knowledge or principles for successful, wise living]_:

_____

_____

_____

7 God wants <u>me</u> to ❏ agree with ❏ believe, ❏ choose, ❏ desire, ❏ do, ❏ follow, ❏ have, ❏ possess, ❏ take action on, and/or ❏ understand _this_:

_____

_____

_____

8 My biggest challenge in being an "influence" at this time is:

_____

_____

_____

9 As an "influencer," I am concerned about:

_____

_____

_____

10 The verse I chose caused me to experience feeling:

❏ alert	❏ elated	❏ excited	❏ happy	❏ optimistic
❏ calm	❏ content	❏ relaxed	❏ serene	❏ tender
❏ bored	❏ depressed	❏ fatigued	❏ grieved	❏ sad
❏ angry	❏ anxious	❏ irritated	❏ stressed	❏ tense	❏ upset

❏ other: _____

for ❏ myself, ❏ my loved one _because:_

_____

_____

_____

Express it

RenewingLives.com

REAP *[to gather, obtain, or receive a reward or benefit from exertions; the fruit of labor or works.]*
Journal *[a record of experiences, ideas, or reflections meant for private use.]*

Read & Rewrite *Book:* Genesis   **EXAMPLE** *Chapter:* 4

|Read To understand the context,[a] I read the ❑ entire chapter above. ⤴
I chose to focus on the verse(s) written below.   *Verse#:* 6-7

6 And the Lord said to Cain, Why are you wroth? and why
is your countenance fallen? 7 If you do well, shall you not be
accepted? and if you do not well, sin lies at the door. And to you
shall be his desire, and you shall rule over him. Gen 4:6-7 KJT

[a]Context *[the passages of scripture which are near the text, either before it or after it.
The sense of a passage of scripture is often illustrated by the context.]*

2 Rewrite the same verses from step **|** in either or both styles:
   ❑ Insert brief definitions (in parenthesis) ❑ Use a different translation

_____

_____

_____

_____

_____

_____

_____

_____

_____

_____

_____

Something I'd like to research further or later:_____

_____ ☞

Express it

REAP Journal: Examine—Inquire into circumstances, facts, and truth to form a correct judgment or opinion. **Judgment** means the determination of the mind formed from comparing the relations of ideas or the comparison of facts and arguments to ascertain truth. **Opinion** means the decision the mind forms of truth or falsehood (which is supported by a degree of evidence that renders it probable but does not produce absolute knowledge or certainty). Research[b] something you find curious or interesting from *anything in the chapter*. Record evidence[c] and resources:

☑ Commentary   ☑ Concordance   ☐ Translation used   ☑ Cross-ref source
Matthew Henry   Strong's   KJV, NKJV   Treasury of SK

☐ Dictionary   ☐ Lexicon   ☐ Other   ☐ Website
                                          Use any resource

☐ I do not have Bible study tools or resources—*here are **my** observations:*

MH—Gen 4:7 God is here reasoning with Cain, to convince him of the sin and folly of his anger and discontent, and to bring him into a good temper again, that further mischief might be prevented. It is an instance of God's patience and condescending goodness that he would deal thus tenderly with so bad a man, in so bad an affair.

• James 1:12-15 Blessed is the man who endures temptation: for when he has been approved, he will receive the crown of life which the Lord has promised to those who love Him. 13 Let no one say when he is tempted, "I am tempted by God": for God cannot be tempted by evil, nor does He Himself tempt anyone. 14 But each one is tempted when he is drawn away by his own desires and enticed. 15 Then, when desire has conceived, it gives birth to sin: and sin, when it is full-grown, brings forth death. NKJV

• Proverbs 28:13 He who covers his sins will not prosper, But whoever confesses and forsakes them will have mercy. NKJV

[b]Research *[to investigate exhaustively: facts, information, or principles in the diligent search for accuracy and truth.]* [c]Evidence *[that which enables the mind to clearly apprehend and be convinced of truth by proof arising from our own perceptions by the senses, from the testimony of others, from inductions of reason, or that which is obvious to the understanding.]*

Express it

RenewingLives.com

REAP Journal: Examine— *(continued)* **EXAMPLE**

• God's Holy Spirit convinces us of sin. If we do right, what we do will be accepted, but sin is always lurking, waiting to tempt us away from God's laws/precepts and consequently robbing us of His blessings (benefits).

• 1 John 1:9 If we confess our sins, he is faithful and just to forgive us our sins, and to cleanse us from all unrighteousness. KJV

• The God-given emotion of anger has a purpose. It awakens energy to solve a problem or gain control of a threatening situation.

• Emotions are involuntary mental reactions that move our mind to excitement. Feelings, compelled by emotions, are influenced by our beliefs, personal experiences, and thoughts. Feelings arouse passion (moving us to action) in positive or negative ways.

Write anything you find interesting

Facts/truths impressed upon my heart from this study of God's word:

• God sees our emotions, attitude, and actions.
• Doing well brings acceptance.   *List Biblical truths you notice*
• We are to rule over/govern our desires and temptations.

I can defend this biblically based ☑Judgment *(certain)* ☐ Opinion *(probable)*:

Anger is an emotion that can lead you into bad feelings and thoughts, followed by bad actions and consequences.

Optional—To debate, defend, or discuss ☞

Express it

REAP Journal: Acknowledge & Attest— (anything in the chapter)

Acknowledge—I sense God wants me to:
☑ Admit ☐ Avoid ☐ Believe ☐ Follow ☐ Heed ☑ Notice ☐ Obey ☐ Receive
☑ Realize the truths listed below as a review from my study of God's word:

I need to rule over sin and not allow feelings from anger control of my freedom and future. God lovingly reminded Cain that he could choose a different mindset and avoid allowing sin to rule him. I have the same choice, daily!

• Heed God's warning that "sin lies at the door. And you shall be his desire". Be careful you don't let ungodly "feelings" rule you.

• Read God's word daily to get His perspective on everything.

• Sin should not have ruling power over a Believer's life. As a Christian, I have God's Holy Spirit living inside me. If I ask, God will help me overcome feelings that conflict with His teaching. I need to trust in Him more than my heart or feelings.

Note how God's word has affected you

Spiritually, **REAP** communicates action and consequences.
Please *the flesh*—reap corruption. Please *the Lord*—reap eternal life.
This hour, my ☐ actions ☐ thoughts... ☐ pleased *the flesh* ☐ pleased *the Lord*.

Express it

RenewingLives.com

R E A P Journal: Acknowledge & Attest— *(anything in the chapter)*

2 Attest—Here is an event, experience, incident, observation, or occurrence that left an impression on me (good or bad), which <u>bears witness, or supports</u> <u>the truth, facts, or other evidence</u> in the ☐ chapter or ☑ verse(s): _____

☐ I heard/read/viewed something <u>which seemed credible</u> (name the book, Internet, magazine, movie, music, newspaper, radio, television, etc.):

_____

☑ I personally (eye witness), or ☐ someone I know experienced this:

My flesh desires to suck me into exploring and expounding on bad thoughts which leads to bad actions. Share with my small group about the time I was stuck on bad thoughts and "told off" my husband. How wrong that was, so much so that it still easily comes to mind as a regret in life. Even though that's true, I still struggle to day with the same thing. Anger doesn't fix problems, it creates new ones. *Share anything relevant*

E x p r e s s i t

EXAMPLE

R E A P Journal: **Pray**— ("talk" to God on paper)   **EXAMPLE**

Pray—Write out a prayer of your heart to including one or more of:
☑**A**doration/honor/praise/respect ☑**C**onfession ☑**T**hankfulness ☑**S**upplication

Supplication *[to earnestly and humbly request God's aid]* includes:
❑ **B**lessing/benefits ☑**F**orgiveness ❑ **G**race ☑**I**ntervention ❑ **M**ercy ❑ **P**eace

Lord, you ARE all-knowing. I confess I struggle with not ruling over
my thought life. I need help, and it is only a prayer away. Please
help me to rely on your word and talk to you more. Thank you for
providing Your Holy Spirit and convincing me of sin. I want the good
you have for me, not the consequences of my sin. You know the
prayer of my heart is that my children, grandchildren, and loved ones
receive You.

Spiritual Goal: Memorize this—think on good things!
Philippians 4:8 Finally, brethren, whatsoever things are true,
whatsoever things are honest, whatsoever things are just,
whatsoever things are pure, whatsoever things are lovely,
whatsoever things are of good report: if there be any virtue,
and if there be any praise, think on these things.

Diary note: This date in 1963 is when my mom realized for the first
time she couldn't control things—it eventually led to her accepting Christ.

E x p r e s s   i t

Renewinglives.com

REAP *[to gather, obtain, or receive a reward or benefit from exertions; the fruit of labor or works.]*
Journal *[a record of experiences, ideas, or reflections meant for private use.]*

Read & Rewrite *Book:* _____ *Chapter:* ___

I Read To understand the context,[a] I read the ❏ entire chapter above. ↰
I chose to focus on the verse(s) written below.   *Verse#:* _____

_____

_____

_____

[a]Context *[the passages of scripture which are near the text, either before it or after it.*
The sense of a passage of scripture is often illustrated by the context.]

2 Rewrite the same verses from step **I** in either or both styles:
❏ Insert brief definitions (in parenthesis) ❏ Use a different translation

_____

_____

_____

_____

_____

_____

_____

_____

_____

_____

Something I'd like to research further or later: _____

☞

_____

Excerpt from: "Read, Write & REAP" (available Online or through your local bookstore).

Express it

REAP Journal: Examine—Inquire into circumstances, facts, and truth to form a correct judgment or opinion. **Judgment** means the determination of the mind formed from comparing the relations of ideas or the comparison of facts and arguments to ascertain truth. **Opinion** means the decision the mind forms of truth or falsehood (which is supported by a degree of evidence that renders it probable but does not produce absolute knowledge or certainty). Research[b] something you find curious or interesting from *anything in the chapter*. Record evidence[c] and resources:

❏ *Commentary*   ❏ *Concordance*   ❏ *Translation used*   ❏ *Cross-ref source*

_____

❏ *Dictionary*   ❏ *Lexicon*   ❏ *Other*   ❏ *Website*

_____

❏ I do not have Bible study tools or resources—*here are* **my** *observations:*

_____
_____
_____
_____
_____
_____
_____
_____
_____
_____
_____
_____
_____
_____

[b]Research *[to investigate exhaustively: facts, information, or principles in the diligent search for accuracy and truth.]* [c]Evidence *[that which enables the mind to clearly apprehend and be convinced of truth by proof arising from our own perceptions by the senses, from the testimony of others, from inductions of reason, or that which is obvious to the understanding.]*

Express it

RenewingLives.com

REAP Journal: Examine— *(continued)*

_____
_____
_____
_____
_____
_____
_____
_____
_____
_____
_____
_____
_____
_____
_____
_____
_____

Facts/truths impressed upon my heart from this study of God's word:

● _____

● _____

● _____

I can defend this biblically based ❑ **Judgment** *(certain)* ❑ **Opinion** *(probable)*:

_____

_____

Express it

REAP Journal: Acknowledge & Attest— *(anything in the chapter)*

I Acknowledge—I sense God wants me to:

❏ Admit ❏ Avoid ❏ Believe ❏ Follow ❏ Heed ❏ Notice ❏ Obey ❏ Receive
❏ Realize the truths listed below as a review from my study of God's word:

_____

_____

_____

_____

_____

_____

_____

_____

_____

_____

_____

_____

_____

_____

_____

_____

_____

_____

Spiritually, **REAP** communicates action and consequences.
Please *the flesh*—reap corruption. Please *the Lord*—reap eternal life.
This hour, my ❏ actions ❏ thoughts... ❏ pleased *the flesh* ❏ pleased *the Lord*.

Express it

RenewingLives.com

R E A P Journal: Acknowledge & Attest— *(anything in the chapter)*

2 Attest—Here is an event, experience, incident, observation, or occurrence that left an impression on me (good or bad), which <u>bears witness, or supports the truth, facts, or other evidence</u> in the ❏ chapter or ❏ verse(s): _____

❏ I heard/read/viewed something <u>which seemed credible</u> (name the book, Internet, magazine, movie, music, newspaper, radio, television, etc.):

_____

❏ I personally (eye witness), or ❏ someone I know experienced this:

_____
_____
_____
_____
_____
_____
_____
_____
_____
_____
_____
_____
_____
_____
_____
_____
_____
_____

Express it

REAP Journal: Pray— *("talk" to God on paper)*

Pray—Write out a prayer of your heart to including one or more of:
❑ **A**doration/honor/praise/respect ❑ **C**onfession ❑ **T**hankfulness ❑ **S**upplication

Supplication *[to earnestly and humbly request God's aid]* includes:
❑ **B**lessing/benefits ❑ **F**orgiveness ❑ **G**race ❑ **I**ntervention ❑ **M**ercy ❑ **P**eace

_____

_____

_____

_____

_____

_____

_____

_____

_____

_____

_____

_____

_____

_____

_____

_____

_____

Diary note: _____

_____

Express it

RenewingLives.com

Memory Verse

Express it

Express it

RenewingLives.com

Sin in the Bible

Sin—noun *[to miss the mark (and so not share in the prize); bear the blame; trespass; whatever is contrary to God's commands or law (lawlessness); an offense and its penalty; the voluntary departure of one who has the power to act from a known rule of rectitude/ rightness or duty prescribed by God (rebellion); any voluntary transgression or violation of the divine law or command; a wicked act; iniquity; sin implies not action only but neglect of known duty, all evil thoughts, purposes, words, and desires.]*

Sin **might** be introduced by the words: *abominable, abomination, abusers, adultery, afraid, afflict the just, anger, angry, arrogance, ashamed, backbiters, bitterness, blasphemers, blasphemy, boasting, boasters, brawling, busybody, carnal minded, chambering, clamor, complainers, conceit, contentious, corrupt, covenantbreakers, covet, covetous, covetousness, crafty, crime, cunning craftiness, cursing, damnation, deceit, debt, defile, defraud, despise chastening, despiteful, dishonest, dishonesty, disobedience, disobedient, despisers of those that are good, divination, divisions, doubletongued, drunkenness, effeminate, enchanter, enmity, emulations, entice, envy, envying, error, evil, evil concupiscence, evil eye, evil thoughts, evildoer, evildoing, extortion, false accusers, false prophets, false teachers, false report, false witness, fault, fearful, fierce, filthiness, filthy conversation, filthy lucre, fleshly, foolish talking, foolishness, fornication, greed, greediness, glutton, guile, guilt, guilty, harlot, hasty, hate, hateful, hatred, haters, haters of God, heady, highminded, heresies, hypocrisy, idle words, idolaters, idolatry, implacable, incontinent, iniquity, inordinate affection, inventors of evil, jesting, judging, kill, killing, lasciviousness, liars, lie, lovers of pleasure, lovers of their own selves, lust, lying, malicious, maliciousness, malignity, mock, murder, murderers, murmuring, not given to wine, old wives fables, offence, pride, profane, proud, provoking, puffed up, purloining, quarrel, railing, rebellion, reveling, riot, rioting, riotous, seditions, slander, slay, sluggard, smite, sorcery, steal, stealing, stiff necked, striker, strife, swearing, swearing falsely, take a bribe, thief, traitors, transgressed, transgression, trespassed, trucebreakers, trusting in riches, turn aside the poor, unbelief, unbelieving, uncleanness, unforgiving, ungodliness, ungodly, unholy, unmerciful, unrighteous, unrighteousness, unthankful, vainglory, vain jangling, variance, wantonness, whisperers, whore, whoredom, whoremongers, wicked, wickedness, witch, witchcraft, without natural affection, without understanding, worldly, wrath, wrong (and many more words in the Bible.)*

Express it

Sin is a generic term for <u>any</u> violation of God's commands and/or law. **"For all have sinned, and come short of the glory of God;"** *Romans 3:23*

Sin can be accidental, unintentional, and even unknown to the sinner, *or* deliberate, intentional, and/or presumptuous *[arrogant; proud; unduly confident to excess; willful; done with bold design, rash confidence, or in violation of known duty]*.

Sin is committed by:

Commission—any intentional or unintentional act, thought, or word we do, say, or think that violates God's commands and/or law. Though they had been commanded otherwise, Adam and Eve intentionally disobeyed God: **"And when the woman saw that the tree was good for food, and that it was pleasant to the eyes, and a tree to be desired to make one wise, she took of the fruit thereof, and did eat, and gave also to her husband with her; and he did eat."** Genesis 3:6

Omission—any act, thought, or word we fail to do or say when we should have. **"Therefore to him that knows to do good, and does it not, to him it is sin."** James 4:17

Types of sin include:

Trespass—intentional or unintentional deviation from the boundaries, commands, and/or laws of God.

Transgression—willful disobedience, purposeful trespassing, rebellion against, or the blatant disregard of, the boundaries, commands, and/or laws of God.

Iniquity—a deliberate, willful, premeditated choice to violate the boundaries, commands, and/or laws of God, and to do so without reverence or respect of God, fear of the consequences of sin, or change of mind from wrong to right—the evidence a reprobate *[unapproved; worthless (literally or morally); rejected]* mind.

Ask God to forgive you—Read John 3
"For God so loved the world, that he gave his only begotten Son, that whosoever believes in him should not perish, but have everlasting life. For God sent not his Son into the world to condemn the world; but that the world through him might be saved." John 3:16-17

Express it

Renewing Lives.com

Sin *(continued)*

List some of the violations of God's commands, law, etc., within the chapter, then categorize and share your comments.

Sc=Sin of commission, So=Sin of omission
T=Trespass, Tr=Transgression, In=Iniquity

C/V#

_____ | _____

_____

_____

_____

_____ ❑ Sc *or* ❑ So: ❑ T ❑ Tr ❑ In

_____ | _____

_____

_____

_____ ❑ Sc *or* ❑ So: ❑ T ❑ Tr ❑ In

_____ | _____

_____

_____

_____ ❑ Sc *or* ❑ So: ❑ T ❑ Tr ❑ In

_____ | _____

_____

_____

_____ ❑ Sc *or* ❑ So: ❑ T ❑ Tr ❑ In

Express it

Sin *(continued)*

Sc=Sin of commission, So=Sin of omission
T=Trespass, Tr=Transgression, In=Iniquity

C/V#

_____ |_____

_____

_____

_____

_____

_____ ❏ Sc *or* ❏ So: ❏ T ❏ Tr ❏ In

_____ |_____

_____

_____

_____

_____ ❏ Sc *or* ❏ So: ❏ T ❏ Tr ❏ In

Of the sins you listed, which one can you most relate to and why?

_____

_____

_____

_____

Psalm 1 should cause you to realize the seriousness of sin. Fortunately we have God's remedy. What is it according to John 3:16-17?

_____

_____

_____

_____

Express it

RenewingLives.com

State+See+Signify=Stirred

Read and choose ❏ *one* verse ❏ a few *connected/related* verses to write about:

Book: _____ Chapter: _____ Verse(s): _____

❏ ASV ❏ CSB ❏ ESV ❏ KJV ❏ KJT ❏ NASB ❏ NIV ❏ NKJV ❏ NLT ❏ _____

1 What does the verse you chose **STATE** *[express in words]*?

_____

_____

_____

_____

_____

_____

2 What do you **SEE** *[perceive; observe; notice; know; attend or look to; regard; feel; experience; learn; comprehend; discern; have intellectual sight; understand; have a full understanding of]*?

_____

_____

_____

_____

_____

_____

3 What does the verse **SIGNIFY** *[indicate; direct your mind to; mean]*?

_____

_____

_____

_____

_____

_____

☞

Express it

State+See+Signify=Stirred (continued)

4 Knowing what God's word states, what you see, and what it signifies, what could/should/would you do? To what action is your heart/mind **STIRRED** [to animate or put into motion; to agitate, excite, incite, move, prompt to action; to instigate by inflaming passions; to make more lively or vigorous; as, to stir up the mind; to quicken (to make alive; to revive or resuscitate, as from death or an inanimate state)]?

_____

_____

_____

_____

_____

_____

_____

_____

_____

_____

_____

_____

_____

_____

_____

_____

_____

_____

Express it

RenewingLives.com

Struggle—noun *[properly, to strive, or to make efforts with a twisting or with contortions of the body, hence, to use great efforts; to contend; to labor hard in pain or anguish or any kind of difficulty or distress; to be in agony; to make forcible effort to obtain an object, or to avoid an evil; contest; contention; strife; contortions of extreme distress.]*

1 This is my most difficult personal **struggle:**

_____

_____

_____

_____

_____

_____

_____

_____

_____

_____

_____

_____

_____

_____

_____

_____

_____

_____

_____

_____

Express it

Struggle *(continued)*

_____

_____

_____

_____

_____

_____

_____

_____

_____

_____

_____

2 My family, friends, and loved ones have been affected by ***this***:

_____

_____

3 I can celebrate these victories *[advantage or superiority gained over appetites (the natural desire of pleasure or good), passions, spiritual enemies, or temptations.]*

_____

_____

_____

4 What I will do to draw closer to God and His word for help and comfort:

_____

_____

_____

Express it

RenewingLives.com

Name: _____ Date __/__/____

Study Buddy/Friend: _____

Address _____

City/State/Zip _____

Phone/Cell _____

Email _____

Other _____

Date/How/Where we met _____

Notes _____

Study Buddy/Friend: _____

Address _____

City/State/Zip _____

Phone/Cell _____

Email _____

Other _____

Date/How/Where we met _____

Notes _____

Study Buddy/Friend: _____

Address _____

City/State/Zip _____

Phone/Cell _____

Email _____

Other _____

Date/How/Where we met _____

Notes _____

Express it

Study Buddy/Friend: _____

Address _____

City/State/Zip _____

Phone/Cell _____

Email _____

Other _____

Date/How/Where we met _____

Notes _____

Study Buddy/Friend: _____

Address _____

City/State/Zip _____

Phone/Cell _____

Email _____

Other _____

Date/How/Where we met _____

Notes _____

Study Buddy/Friend: _____

Address _____

City/State/Zip _____

Phone/Cell _____

Email _____

Other _____

Date/How/Where we met _____

Notes _____

Express it

RenewingLives.com

Survey Query —verb transitive *[to examine by questions; to seek; to inquire.]*

Surveys are used to gain insight into various topics. The information is tallied to come to an understanding of the feeling, judgment, or opinion of others.

True False

1 _____

_____ ❏ ❏

2 _____

_____ ❏ ❏

3 _____

_____ ❏ ❏

4 _____

_____ ❏ ❏

5 _____

_____ ❏ ❏

6 _____

_____ ❏ ❏

7 _____

_____ ❏ ❏

8 _____

_____ ❏ ❏

9 _____

_____ ❏ ❏

10 _____

_____ ❏ ❏

11 _____

_____ ❏ ❏

Express it

Survey Query *(continued)*

12 _____

_____ ☐ ☐

13 _____

_____ ☐ ☐

14 _____

_____ ☐ ☐

15 _____

_____ ☐ ☐

16 _____

_____ ☐ ☐

17 _____

_____ ☐ ☐

18 _____

_____ ☐ ☐

19 _____

_____ ☐ ☐

20 _____

_____ ☐ ☐

21 _____

_____ ☐ ☐

22 _____

_____ ☐ ☐

23 _____

_____ ☐ ☐

Express it

RenewingLives.com

God's word **Made Personal**—adjective [relating to an individual; affecting individuals; peculiar or proper to him or her, or to private actions or character.]

From the book you are studying, choose: ❏ *one* verse ❏ a few *connected/related* verses or ❏ *one* chapter to make personal:

I considered chapter/verse(s): _____ then chose: ____

Hand copy the chapter/verse(s) you chose to ponder on the lines that follow, but insert YOUR name whenever it is possible to personally apply to an individual. For example:

"Blessed is (insert your name) **that walks not in the counsel of the ungodly, nor stands in the way of sinners, nor sits in the seat of the scornful. But** (insert your name) **delight is in the law of the LORD; and in his law does** (insert your name) **meditate day and night."** Psalm 1:1-2

Book: _____ Chapter: _____ Verse(s): _____

_____

_____

_____

_____

_____

_____

_____

_____

_____

_____

_____

_____

_____

_____

_____

☞

Express it

The Word Made Personal *(continued)*

_____

_____

_____

_____

_____

_____

_____

_____

_____

_____

_____

_____

_____

_____

_____

_____

_____

_____

_____

❏ ASV ❏ CSB ❏ ESV ❏ KJV ❏ NASB ❏ NIV ❏ NKJV ❏ NLT ❏ _____

Express it

RenewingLives.com

Name: _____ Date __/__/____

T-Shirt Art
Inspired by something *from the chapter,* create a T-Shirt design that is wholesome *[contributing to the health of the mind; favorable to morals, religion or prosperity; conducive to public happiness, virtue, or peace].*

Front

Express it

T-Shirt Art *(continued)*

Back

Express it

RenewingLives.com

What did I learn...—verb *[to acquire or gain ideas, information, instruction, intelligence, knowledge, or skill of something before unknown.]*

1 ...about death, life, or my eternal destiny? _____

_____

_____

2 ...about God's character, desires, plans, priorities, promises, warnings, ways, etc.? _____

_____

_____

3 ...about God's grace, mercy, and plan of redemption? _____

_____

_____

4 ...about God's standards of right and wrong? _____

_____

_____

5 ...about my fallen condition/sinful nature? _____

_____

_____

6 ...about myself? _____

_____

_____

7 ...about this world, it's people or ways? _____

_____

_____

8 ...that affects my involvement and relationship with my church? ____

_____

_____

_____

Express it

What did I learn? *(continued)*

9 ...that affects my relationship with other believers? _____

_____

_____

10 ...that caused me to be encouraged? _____

_____

_____

11 ...that changed my thinking? _____

_____

_____

12 ...that confirms God's love to me? _____

_____

_____

13 ...that I need to put into practice? _____

_____

_____

14 ...that I should respond to with obedience? _____

_____

_____

15 ...that I want to pray on or about more often? _____

_____

_____

16 ...that will change how I live moving forward? _____

_____

_____

17 ...that will help me reach out to my unbelieving family or friends? ____

_____

_____

Express it

RenewingLives.com

Word Search A— Psalm 1

Search up, down, forward, backward, or diagonally for words from the Psalm. When you discover a word spelled correctly, use a pencil to lightly draw a line through all its letters, or circle the entire word. I found: _____

```
W J O R O F T L U S J S H A L L H T S E A T O U G
A O T H E O S A N A C Y L S D R I V E S H L I W N
Y K N O W S H W G S N O R I G K D T W W E T S N N
S T A N D S A X O R O T R N D M A H L U T H F O O
L E A F M F L T D T A H H N N E Y E Q Z H A B O T
U A R E M V L H L T L N C E F O L B U T E T U H R
N Z B I N W F E Y H H W D R R U R I G H T E O U S
I T E F W H I C H E J I A S O I L V G R F O R T H
G I H T N O T I N D N T S I F N T H E H H I S T U
H V S E U I M A N O W H U P L A N T E D T P G O N
T B Z P T H A T O E A E R I V E R S K C H A F F G
H L U R R E X A T S Y R F I T P B L E S S E D O O
E O T T I O U N G O D L Y I S H L M O F Z W I S D
B R H H L G S D W W H C O N G R E G A T I O N H L
R D E E A K H P L H E D O E S V B A N D S H Z A Y
I T O Q W B N T E U A E Z C J O Y T R E E E R L P
N H F L S I N N E R S T U C O U A M A L N W G L R
G E B I T Q W K I O B H S N I U D S E G O O I E A
S R S K F R U I T N U E S O G N N G T D K R T N N
Q H H E H S H A L L I S T H E O N S M A I N D A D
W I A Z I B E Y S P E R I S H V D X E E N T N O R
A S L O S W T H E R E F O R E H E L P L N D A Z J
T W L F Q I A R E B I C A T H E I R Y H Q T W T M
E A L I K E T V O U S E A S O N R S X T H E A H E
R Y P T H E I S F T F C O F P W A L K S N Y Y E T
```

Word Search B— Psalm 1

Search up, down, forward, backward, or diagonally for words from the Psalm. When you discover a word spelled correctly, use a pencil to lightly draw a line through all its letters, or circle the entire word. I found: _____

```
W O K N O T O Z W A R K N O R B E W H I C H H T T
A F I L E A F F W A F I F J S B U T V I N T R R H
Y U N G O D L Y M N Y O G S U C V D R I V E S E E
E F O R T H H T N T K T R H I D O S W A T E R E R
S H A L L R U E H O H H P U T T G R R I V E R S K
U R D O E S T N I E T E C L D E S M N E Q B D R P
R I G H T E O U S N Q T C O A E O F E F W U T H E
S F Q S U N G O D L Y H T O U N L U R N U T H C R
R I D V T X O D O E S E H U N N T I S U T L E S I
K N O W S A B O F S G O E N I G S E G U I B L I S
P A N D K A N U L N H F B G N I R E D H M T A N H
T S O L H S T D T I O A Y O A N D E L C T E W N A
B H T T I T H H S B K R L D T A T O G W H X Z E N
C A E L S T Y A E P T E I L O H F H F A I A B R D
N L L O R D I H L H B H N Y I I E A E T T N F S D
J L T H E H G J I L F R E V W N Y W F R H I D F A
T Q H M I I I Y S M E D I T A T E A S R E E O T R
E B A W H A T S O E V E R N T C S Y E O J F N N E
S O T D A Y R M L D V H H L G M I L A F M S O P U
T T F A S E A T B E X G E O H S N I S T G A R R T
A H U N L J U Q S H A L L R I N N K O W H I N O E
N E E D O S L W I T H E R D S O E E N I A A N S I
D N H I S Q O S J I W A L K S O R X Y N B Y T P T
Z N I G H T N O T H E L A W D O S H I S A R E E H
R A B L E S S E D H I S O O F U N G O D L Y B R E
```

Test Yourself

Once you complete the study of Psalm 1 you will be able to answer the following questions with confidence. Choose the most biblically correct answer to each question.

1 The book of Psalms contain:
  A ❑ Poems, parables
  B ❑ Proverbs, poems
  C ❑ Songs, parables
  D ❑ Songs, poems

2 This acronym is biblically sound:
  A ❑ **P**lease **R**espond **A**nd **Y**ell it
  B ❑ **P**lease **R**espond **A**nswer **Y**es
  C ❑ **P**lease **R**espond **A**lways **Y**es
  D ❑ **P**lease **R**espond **A**nswer **Y**our will

3 Psalm 1 compares:
  A ❑ Chaff with leaves
  B ❑ Fruit and trees
  C ❑ The rich and the poor
  D ❑ The righteous and unrighteous

4 Psalm 1 begins with:
  A ❑ A beatitude
  B ❑ A benediction
  C ❑ An Invocation
  D ❑ Thanksgiving

5 Blessed means:
  A ❑ Good things are coming my way
  B ❑ Financially rich
  C ❑ O how happy
  D ❑ Well off

6 The godly are compared to:
  A ❑ A leaf
  B ❑ A tree
  C ❑ Fruit
  D ❑ Rivers of water

7 The ungodly does not
  A ❑ Care to be blessed
  B ❑ Sit in the seat of the scornful
  C ❑ Stand in the way of sinners
  D ❑ Walk in ungodly counsel

8 Delight is defined as:
  A ❑ Care, concern
  B ❑ Light, unconcerned
  C ❑ Pleasant, important
  D ❑ Pleasure, desire

9 "The law" in Psalm 1 refers to:
  A ❑ Precepts and Statues
  B ❑ The Decalogue
  C ❑ The Pentateuch
  D ❑ All of the above

10 Biblical Hebrew consists of:
  A ❑ Capital and lowercase letters
  B ❑ Lowercase letters
  C ❑ Punctuation
  D ❑ Uppercase letters

Express it

11 Psalm 1 teaches the LORD is:
A ❏ Deity
B ❏ Eternal
C ❏ The self-existent
D ❏ All of the above

12 The phrase "like a tree" is a:
A ❏ Series
B ❏ Sequence
C ❏ Simile
D ❏ Similitude

13 The definition of meditate includes:
A ❏ To imagine, to mourn
B ❏ To murmur, to ponder
C ❏ To mutter, to roar
D ❏ All of the above

14 A tree represents:
A ❏ Height
B ❏ Power
C ❏ Strength
D ❏ Width

15 In Psalm 1, fruit represents:
A ❏ A busy life
B ❏ A reward
C ❏ Children
D ❏ The garden of Eden

16 Two words with the same sense:
A ❏ Money and means
B ❏ Time and money
C ❏ Times and seasons
D ❏ Seasons and holidays

17 The ungodly shall not:
A ❏ Be able to defend themselves
B ❏ Be acquitted
C ❏ Obtain righteousness
D ❏ All of the above

18 The ungodly are compared to:
A ❏ Hot air
B ❏ Rotten fruit
C ❏ Wind
D ❏ Worthless matter

19 Perish refers to:
A ❏ A city in France
B ❏ Endless misery
C ❏ Immortality
D ❏ None of the above

20 Psalm 1 encourages Believer's:
A ❏ Don't worry, be happy
B ❏ Live righteously
C ❏ Pray for prosperity
D ❏ Pray for world peace

21 If you study the Bible you will:
A ❏ Gain wisdom and knowledge
B ❏ Improve reading, spelling skills
C ❏ Increase English grammar skills
D ❏ All of the above

22 Poetry:
A ❏ Crafts imagery into words
B ❏ Crafts words into imagery
C ❏ Is sound or thought based
D ❏ All of the above

Express it

RenewingLives.com

Test Yourself *(continued)*

23 Opinion means:
A ❑ Absolute certainty & knowledge
B ❑ Don't question me, I'm right!
C ❑ My decision of truth/falsehood
D ❑ What I say, stands!

24 In English grammar, a "figure" is:
A ❑ A form or shape
B ❑ Arithmetic like 1, 2, 3, etc.
C ❑ An unnatural word or sentence
D ❑ The steps of a dancer

25 There are __ "figures of speech":
A ❑ 8
B ❑ 11
C ❑ 12
D ❑ 217

26 An advocate:
A ❑ Holds hatred in the heart
B ❑ Is entertained by injuring others
C ❑ Makes you feel oppressed
D ❑ Pleads the cause of another

27 Evil people are:
A ❑ Mischievous
B ❑ Unhappy
C ❑ Wicked
D ❑ All of the above

28 Sin means:
A ❑ Bear the blame
B ❑ Miss the mark
C ❑ Neglect of known duty
D ❑ All of the above

29 How many minutes did you spend reading God's word yesterday?
A ❑ None
B ❑ 1-5
C ❑ 6-10
D ❑ 11 or more

30 How would you grade yourself on your Godly actions yesterday?
A ❑ A
B ❑ B-C
C ❑ D
D ❑ F

31 How would you grade yourself on your Godly language yesterday?
A ❑ A
B ❑ B-C
C ❑ D
D ❑ F

32 How would you grade yourself on your Godly thoughts yesterday?
A ❑ A
B ❑ B-C
C ❑ D
D ❑ F

33 How would you rate your desire to learn God's word?
A ❑ None
B ❑ 1 (low)
C ❑ 5 (medium)
D ❑ 10 (high)

Express it

Bullet Points *[used to signify importance; any point worthy of special emphasis.]*

- _____
  _____

- _____
  _____

- _____
  _____

- _____
  _____

- _____
  _____

- _____
  _____

- _____
  _____

- _____
  _____

- _____
  _____

- _____
  _____

- _____

Express it

RenewingLives.com

Express it—Insight, lists, questions, notes, thoughts, etc.

Express it

Praise Report (Side 1 of 2)

❏ Share anything that honors and magnifies the Lord, *OR*
❏ Share what God is showing you as you grow in faith.

_____

_____

_____

_____

_____

_____

_____

_____

_____

_____

_____

_____

_____

_____

_____

_____

_____

_____

_____

_____

_____

_____

_____

Prayer Request

Please pray with me, and for me, about this:

_____

_____

_____

_____

_____

_____

❏ I received Jesus Christ as my Lord and Savior on: _____

Note: We share some letters and responses submitted to our ministry to rally prayer for you and others but blot out identifying information (see exception below.)

❏ I am incarcerated in the USA. I have completed this form myself and mailed it <u>directly from my institution</u>. I would appreciate a Biblically-based book to keep me "Busy in The Bible."™ *(If your loved one is "inside," mail this blank form to them.)*

Language(s) I read fluently *[easily; well]*:	Language(s) I write fluently:
_____	_____

First & Last Name _____

Birthplace_____ Birthdate_____

ID# or Fed A# _____ Housing/Cell _____

Facility Name _____

Facility Address _____

City/State/Zip _____

In addition to sharing letters, etc. (above): OPTIONAL—As an adult, I grant permission to publish, in any form, my name with all or part of my comments (this page front & back) without compensation—allowing editing as needed.

✗ _____

Signature   Name Printed   Date

Mail to: Renewing Lives, PO Box **5529**, Diamond Bar, CA 91765-7529

Has this book made a difference? (Side 1 of 2)

Please share how you found the book: _____
helpful, how God used it to affect you, or how it has made a difference in your life. The personal experiences and testimonies of God working through His word encourages volunteers and supporters of this *ministry by mail* to keep you *Busy in the Bible.*™

_____

_____

_____

_____

_____

_____

_____

_____

_____

_____

_____

_____

_____

_____

_____

_____

_____

_____

_____

_____

Help us help others (Side 2 of 2)

❑ I noticed an error in need of correction, and/or
❑ Here is a comment, idea, or suggestion to make this book better:

_____

_____

❑ Please pray *with me, and for me,* about this:

_____

_____

_____

❑ I received Jesus Christ as my Lord and Savior on: _____

❑ I am incarcerated in the USA. I have completed this form myself and mailed it <u>directly from my institution.</u> I would appreciate a Biblically-based book to keep me "Busy in The Bible."™ *(If your loved one is "inside," mail this blank form to them.)*

Language(s) I read fluently *[easily; well]*:	Language(s) I write fluently:

First & Last Name _____

Birthplace_____ Birthdate _____

ID# or Fed A# _____ Housing/Cell _____

Facility Name _____

Facility Address _____

City/State/Zip _____

Note: We share letters and responses submitted to our ministry to make others aware of needs and encourage prayer support but blot out identifying information (see optional below).

OPTIONAL—As an adult, I grant permission *to publish, in any form,* with all or part of my name and comments (this page front & back) without compensation—allowing editing as needed.

✗
_____
Signature   Name Printed   Date

Mail to: Renewing Lives, PO Box **5529**, Diamond Bar, CA 91765-7529

Made in the USA
Monee, IL
30 December 2021

86657653R00125